First Printing
May 2013

Copyright 2013
Karin Hauschild

Beau Monde Language Services
Florence, Kentucky
USA

Karin Hauschild has many years of
experience teaching a second language,
including English, German and French,
to university students as well as to business executives.
.

She has written several books to help students
synthesize English learning,
in both grammar, in sentence structure
and in academic writing.

She has taught at private language schools
in the US and abroad, and has tutored individuals
in IELTS, TOEFL & TOEIC preparation.

She currently teaches at
Northern Kentucky University.

A Synthesis of English Language Structure

Structure Charts
Exercises
Writing Practice
References

A Synthesis of English Language Structure is designed as an independent study guide for international students of the English language in preparation for TOEFL, IELTS, university placement tests, developmental writing classes, freshman English, and advanced writing classes.

A Synthesis of English Language Structure is comprised of seventeen study units with exercises and answers, writing practice prompts, and reference charts.

A Synthesis of English Language Structure offers three writing reference units with nine essay outlines and annotated sample essays.

Contents

Unit 1	Nouns & Articles	1
Unit 2	Verbs & Tenses	7
Unit 3	Adjectives	15
Unit 4	Adverbs	21
Unit 5	Sentence Structure	27
Unit 6	Transitions	35
Unit 7	Modifiers	41
Unit 8	Gerunds & Infinitives	47
Unit 9	Prepositions	53
Unit 10	Phrasal Verbs	61
Unit 11	Forms	71
Unit 12	Clauses	77
Unit 13	Sentence Combining	83
Unit 14	Parallel Structure	91
Unit 15	Sentence Variety	97

Contents

Unit 16	Idiomatic Expressions	103
Unit 17	Phrases	113
Unit 18	Writing Points	119
Unit 19	Essay Structure	121
Unit 20	Essay Outlines & Sample Essays	125
	Answer Key	155
	Resources	164

Unit 1

Nouns & Articles

Structure Chart
Exercises
Writing Practice
References

Count/Noncount Nouns & Articles

Count Nouns	Noncount Nouns
Single things which can be counted	Categories of objects and concepts which have no plural form

Article Usage

Using a or Ø	*Using a*	*Using the*
Singular Count Nouns — *An orange is sweet.*	Singular Count Nouns — *He bought an apple.*	Singular Count Nouns — *She ate the banana.*
Plural Count Nouns — *Oranges are sweet.*	Plural Count Nouns — *He bought apples.*	Plural Count Nouns — *She ate the bananas.*
Noncount Nouns — *Citrus fruit is good for you.*	Noncount Nouns — *He bought fruit.*	Noncount Nouns — *She ate the fruit.*

Guidelines for Article Usage

Use *a* with non-specific, general nouns. *I know a man.* (one of many men in the world)	Use *the* when talking about a specific thing or something already mentioned. *The man is very kind.* (the specific man already mentioned)	Do not use *the* with a plural count noun or a noncount noun. *Apples are delicious.* *Education is important.* *Honesty is a noble virtue.*

Noncount Nouns

Groups made up of similar items	*Fluids, Solids, Gases & Particles*	*Concepts & Natural Phenomena*
baggage clothing food furniture jewelry mail money scenery traffic	water coffee bread gold paper steam smoke grass sugar	beauty confidence fun honesty weather rain snow wind heat

Use the correct form of the nouns in the box to fill in the blanks.

device	company	path	trail	book

1. New electronic _____ are created every day by various _____.

2. Our side of the mountain has no clear _____ to walk on. There are only overgrown _____ that are difficult to traverse.

3. The local library has many bestseller _____ for residents to borrow anytime they want.

Complete the sentences with the words in the boxes.

4. *flower*

    My patio garden has many _____ growing in it this spring. It is an ever-blooming _____ garden.

5. *house*

    I bought many things for my _____ recently. I consider these things necessary _____ wares.

6. *car*

    He learned how to fix _____ last year. Now he can do _____ repairs quickly.

Complete the sentences with the nouns in the box.

concert	play	tree	traffic	suitcase	luggage

7. I like to go to _____, _____, and movies. I enjoy going out and often go with friends.

8. Because the street has a lot of _____ it has a lot of pedestrian _____.

9. There are _____, carry-on bags and rolling cases waiting for the _____ cart to bring them to the plane.

Complete the sentences with a, an, the, or O.

10. Everyone has _____ problems in _____ life.

11. That book is about _____ adventures of Huckleberry Finn.

12. Wolfgang Amadeus Mozart is _____ name of _____ composer who wrote _____ Requiem. He died at the age of 36 from _____ infection before _____ Requiem could be finished.

13. _____ plants are used in _____ houses and gardens. They provide _____ oxygen and are a source of _____ numerous medicines. We use parts of plants for building _____ houses, making _____ paper and _____ even creating _____ textiles.

14. The ostrich, the biggest bird in the world, eats almost anything, including _____ stones, _____ glass, and _____ other small objects. With its powerful legs, it can kill _____ person with just a single kick.

15. In _____ recent newspaper article, there was an article about _____ swimmer who was saved from _____ shark attack by _____ group of dolphins who chased _____ shark away as it tried to attack. They saved _____ swimmer's life.

Complete the sentences with the singular or plural form of the noun in parentheses.

16. Each of the *(child)* _____ got a present.

17. One of the *(student)* _____ stayed after class to talk to the instructor.

18. All of the *(student)* _____ enjoyed the debate.

19. The instructor was very excited when every *(student)* _____ in the class participated in the discussion.

20. Each of the *(student)* _____ joined the discussion.

Check your answers with the answer key on page 155

Choose a place from the following list.
Choose the one that interests you.
Write about it.

a vacant lot, a city street, a beach, a field of wildflowers, a dark alley, an outdoor market

Use count and noncount nouns with the appropriate articles.
Check correct usage with the structure chart on p. 2.

For editing services, email your writing as a WORD document to:
editessentials@aol.com

Regular & Irregular Plurals

Rule	Examples
Add *s* to most nouns	*bird/birds* *flower/flowers*
Add *es* to nouns ending in *sh, ch, s, z, x*	*beach/beaches* *box/boxes* *breeze/breezes* *bush/bushes*
Change *y* to *i*, add *es*	*baby/babies* *lady/ladies*
Add *es* to some nouns ending in *o*	*echo/echoes* *tomato/tomatoes*
Add *s* to some words ending in *o*	*video/videos* *photo/photos*
Change *f* to *v*, add *es*	*leaf/leaves* *life/lives*
Add *s* to some words ending in *f*	*roof/roofs* *belief/beliefs*
Some words have irregular plural forms	*man/men* *child/children* *woman/women*
Some words are the same in singular and plural	*fish/fish* *series/series*
Words ending in *on* and *um* change *on* and *um* to *a*	*criterion/criteria* *phenomenon/phenomena*
Words ending in *sis* change to *ses*	*thesis/theses* *crisis/crises*

Nouns as Adjectives

A noun in the singular form can be used as an adjective.

She made a fruit salad for the party.

Expressions of Quantity

Expression of Quantity	Used with Count Nouns	Used with Noncount Nouns
one each every	one tree each tree every tree	
two both a couple of a few several many a number of	two trees both trees a couple of trees a few trees several trees many trees a number of trees	
a little much a great deal of		a little coffee much time a great deal of money
no hardly any some a lot of lots of plenty of	no trees hardly any trees some trees a lot of trees lots of trees plenty of trees	no coffee hardly any coffee some coffee a lot of coffee lots of coffee plenty of coffee

Unit 2

Verbs & Tenses

Structure Chart
Exercises
Writing Practice
References

Simple Present	Present Continuous
habitually — NOW	ongoing in the present — NOW
Tom *studies* every day.	Tom *is studying* right now.
Simple Past	**Past Continuous**
in the past — NOW	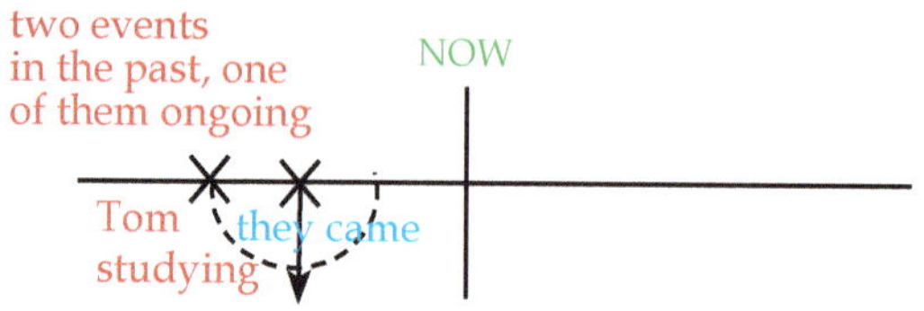 two events in the past, one of them ongoing — NOW
Tom *studied* last night.	Tom *was studying* when they came.
Simple Future	**Future Continuous**
one event in the future — NOW	one event in the future, ongoing — NOW
Tom *will study/is going to study* tomorrow.	Tom *will be/is going to be studying* when they come.

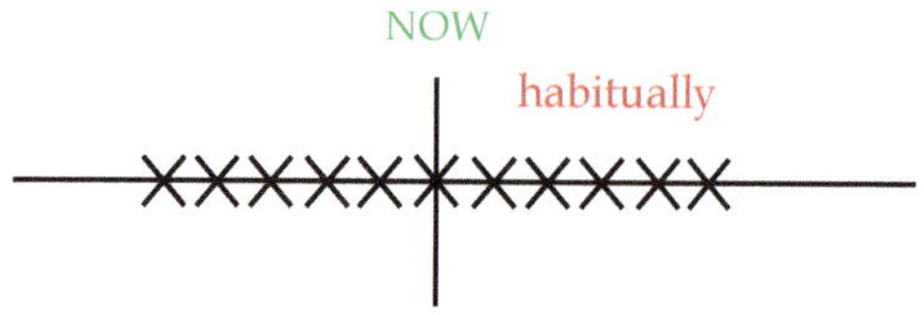

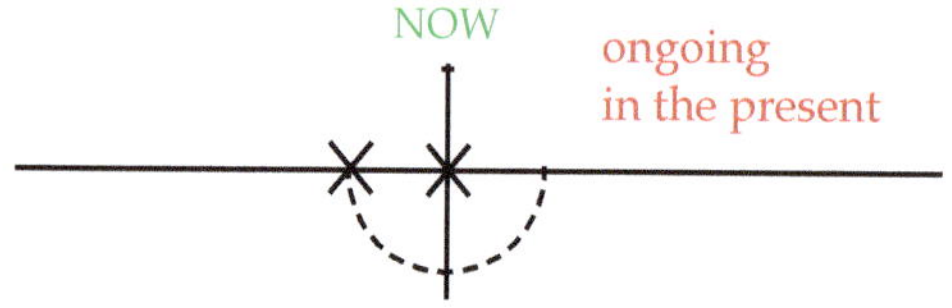

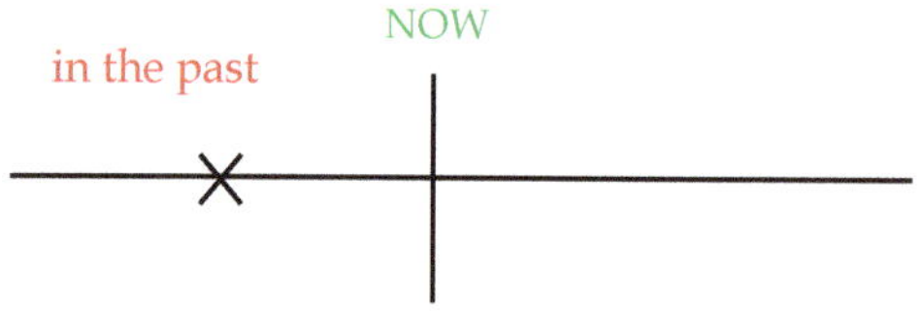

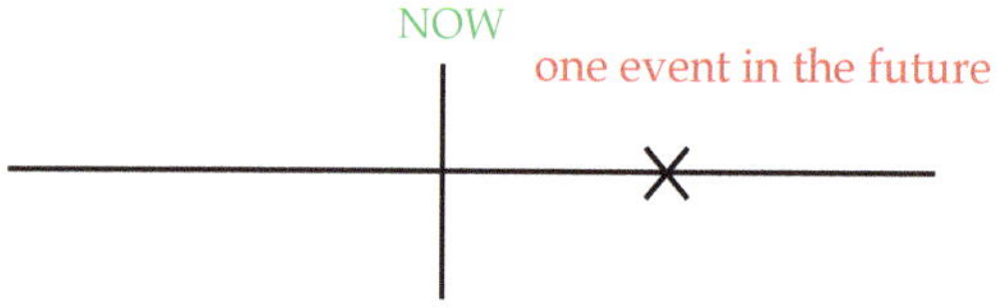

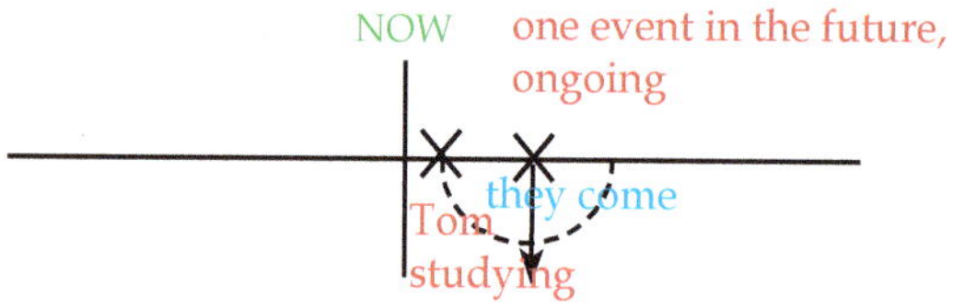

Present Perfect	Present Perfect Continuous
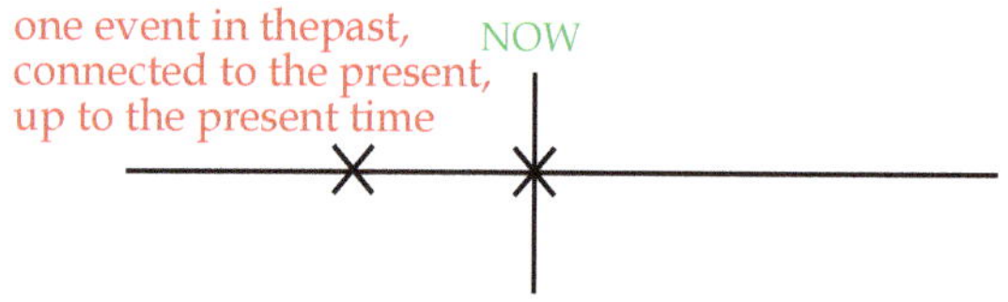 one event in the past, connected to the present, up to the present time — NOW	one event in the past, ongoing to the present, up to the present time — NOW
Tom *has* already *studied* for the test.	Tom *has been studying* for two hours.
Past Perfect	**Past Perfect Continuous**
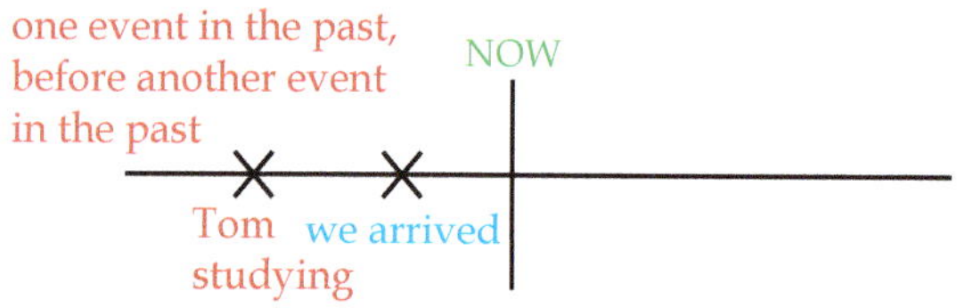 one event in the past, before another event in the past — NOW	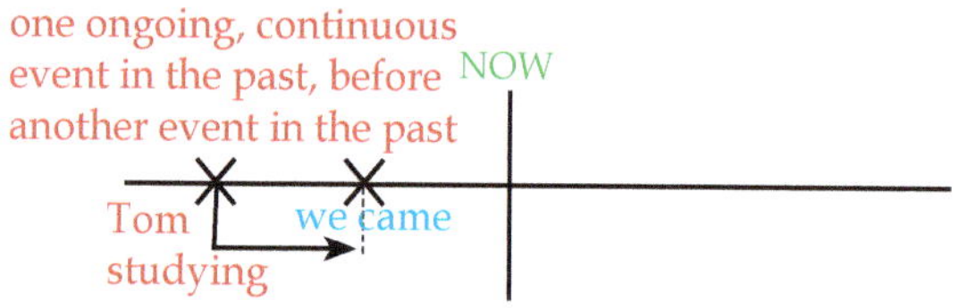 one ongoing, continuous event in the past, before another event in the past — NOW
Tom *had* already *studied* before we arrived.	Tom *had* already *been studying* for two hours before we came.
Future Perfect	**Future Perfect Continuous**
one event in the future, before another event in the future — NOW	one ongoing, continuous event in the future, before another event in the future — NOW
Tom *will* already *have studied* before we arrive.	Tom *will have been studying* for two hours before we arrive.

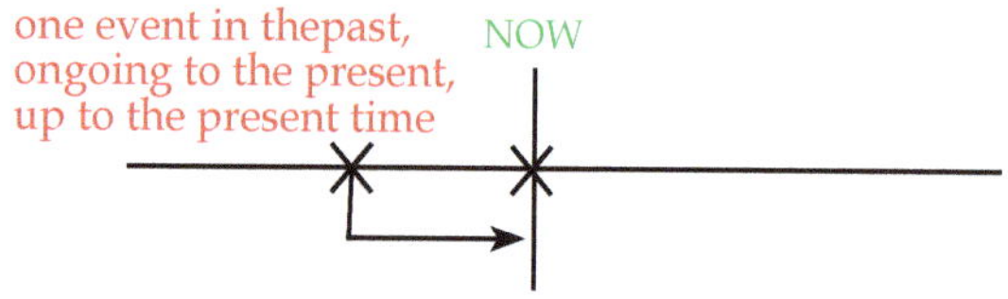

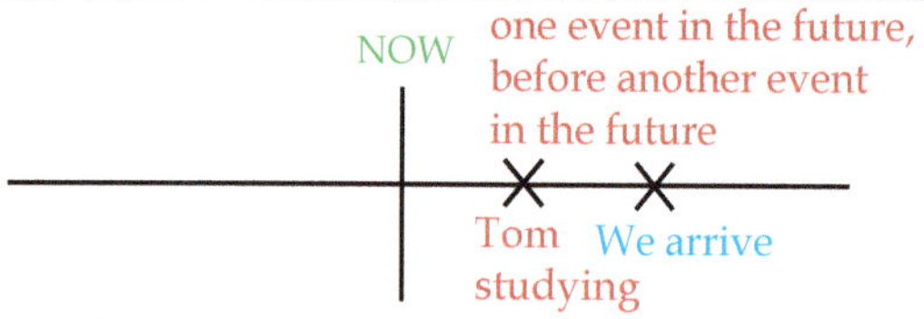

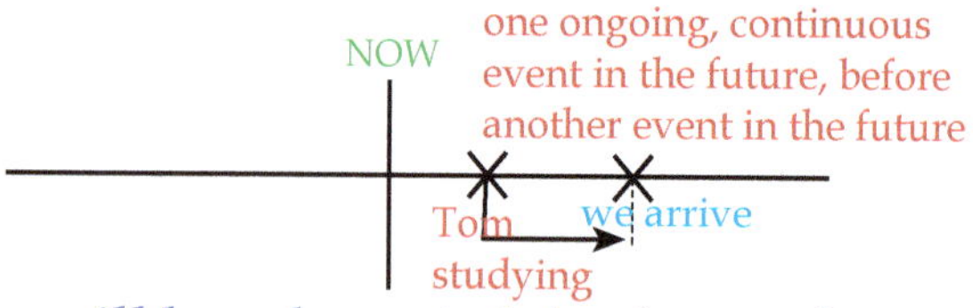

Tense	Usage	Formula	Example
Simple Present	Used for something that is routine or generally true in the present	Verb in present form	He lives in the city. (now)
Simple Past	Used for something that happened in the past	Verb in past form	He lived in the city. (in the past)
Simple Future	Used for something that will happen in the future	Will or Going to + Verb (present)	He will live in the city. (in the future)
Present Continuous	Used for something that is happening in the present in an ongoing way	To Be (present) + Verb + ing	He is living in the city. (at the present time)
Past Continuous	Used for something that happened in the past in an ongoing way	To Be (past) + Verb + ing	He was living in the city. (at some time in the past)
Future Continuous	Used for something that will happen in the future in an ongoing way	Will or Going To + To Be + Verb + ing	He will be living in the city. (at some time in the future)
Present Perfect	Used for an action that happened in the past and may still be happening	Have (present) + Past Participle	He has lived in the city all his life. (he still lives in the city)
Past Perfect	Used for an action that happened in the past before another action in the past	Have (past) + Past Participle	He had lived in the city before he moved to the country. (he no longer lives in the city)
Future Perfect	Used for an action that will have happened in the future before another action in the future	Will + Have (present) + Past Participle	He will have lived in the city before he moves to the country. (at one point he lived in the city)
Present Perfect Continuous	Used for an action that has been happening in the past and may still be happening in an ongoing way	Have (present) + Been + Verb + ing	He has been living in the city all his life. (he is still living in the city)
Past Perfect Continuous	Used for an action that had been happening in an ongoing way in the past and is completely finished	Have (past) + Been + Verb + ing	He had been living in the city all his life. (he is no longer living in the city)
Future Perfect Continuous	Used for an action that will have been happening in an ongoing way in the future before another action in the future	Will + Have (present) + Been + Verb + ing	He will have been living in the city all his life when he moves to the country. (he will no longer be living in the city)

Complete the sentences with the correct tense of the verb in parentheses.

1. Megan and Beth *(study)*_____ French at university this year. They *(study, also)*_____ philosophy. Their classes are *(hold)*_____ every morning of the week.

2. Last week they *(study)*_____ every evening at 8:00. They *(attend, already)*_____ their classes when they *(begin)*_____ to study.

3. They *(always, attend)*_____ class before they *(study)*_____. Each day before they *(go)*_____ to class, they *(read)*._____

4. They *(attend)*_____ class every day in the morning. Yesterday, Beth's mother *(call)*_____ at 10:00, but could *(not, reach)*_____ Beth because Beth *(attend)*_____ French class.

5. Both Megan and Beth *(finish)*_____ two other French classes this semester. Now they *(take)*_____ philosophy. They *(be)*_____ in this class for two semesters. They *(intend)*_____ to finish by spring They *(take)*_____ many courses, but this is the first philosophy course they *(take, ever)*_____.

6. The midwestern US *(experience)*_____ tornadoes every spring. So far, this year, they *(experience)*_____ more than 50 tornadoes. They *(experience)* _____ more storms before summer.

7. Since the weather service *(begin)*_____ to keep records of tornadoes, more than 1000 tornadoes *(occur)*_____ in the central US plains. What *(cause)*_____ tornadoes?

8. The **Wizard of Oz** is a movie about an imaginary tornado that *(show)*_____ what can happen during such a storm.

9. Native American people *(tell)*_____ stories that try to explain storms. They *(say)*_____ that mythical beings *(cause)*_____ weather disturbances.

10. In Asia, there are stories about how to predict tsunamis. In some stories, a tsunami *(depend)*_____ on the phase of the moon. In others, they are the acts of spiritual beings.

11. Although weather forecasters *(know)*_____ a lot these days, they still *(not, can accurately, foretell)*_____ what the weather *(be)*_____ on any given day or in any given season.

12. One of the strongest tsunamis *(happen)*_____ in Japan a few years ago. When the tsunami *(strike)*_____, people *(ride)*_____ on trains, *(work)* _____ in offices, and *(study)*_____ in schools. Suddenly and violently, the whole world *(change)*_____: trains were *(sweep)*_____ to sea and people *(drown)*_____.

13. Many people were *(sweep)*_____ away instantly and *(never, see)*_____ _____ again. Thousands of people *(die)*_____.

14. Can experts *(predict)*_____ tsunamis? Tsunamis *(depend)*_____ on unpredictable forces.

15. Earthquakes in the ocean *(cause, often)*_____ tsunamis. There are warning systems that *(allow)*_____ people to escape the wall of water before it *(reach)*_____ shore. If there *(be)*_____ an early warning system in Thailand, more people would *(be)*_____ saved.

16. There *(seem)*_____ to be no ways of planning for events such as tsunamis.

Choose an action from the following list.
Choose the one that interests you most.
Write about it.

riding a bicycle, crossing a street, shoveling snow, taking a walk, taking a trip, telling a story

Use various tenses in writing your paragraph.
Check correct usage with the structure charts on pp. 8 - 9.
Check the reference chart on pp. 13 - 14 for past tense forms of irregular verbs.

For editing services, email your writing as a WORD document to:
editessentials@aol.com

Irregular Verbs

Group 1
All three groups the same

Simple Form	Simple Past	Past Participle
bet	bet	bet
burst	burst	burst
cost	cost	cost
cut	cut	cut
fit	fit	fit
hit	hit	hit
hurt	hurt	hurt
let	let	let
put	put	put
quit	quit	quit
shut	shut	shut
split	split	split
spread	spread	spread
upset	upset	upset

Group 3
Vowel change from *a* to *u*

Simple Form	Simple Past	Past Participle
begin	began	begun
drink	drank	drunk
ring	rang	rung
run	ran	run
shrink	shrank	shrunk
sing	sang	sung
sink	sank	sunk
swim	swam	swum

Group 4
First and third forms the same

Simple Form	Simple Past	Past Participle
become	became	become
come	came	come
run	ran	run

Group 5
One form very different

Simple Form	Simple Past	Past Participle
be	was, were	been
go	went	gone

Group 2
Past Participle Ending in EN

Simple Form	Simple Past	Past Participle
awake	awoke	awoken
bite	bit	bitten
break	broke	broken
choose	chose	chosen
drive	drove	driven
eat	ate	eaten
fall	fell	fallen
forget	forgot	forgotten
forgive	forgave	forgiven
freeze	froze	frozen
get	got	gotten
give	gave	given
hide	hid	hidden
prove	proved	proven
ride	rode	ridden
rise	rose	risen
shake	shook	shaken
speak	spoke	spoken
steal	stole	stolen
swell	swelled	swollen
take	took	taken
wake	woke	woken
write	wrote	written

Group 6
Past Participle adds N to the simple form

Simple Form	Simple Past	Past Participle
blow	blew	blown
draw	drew	drawn
grow	grew	grown
know	knew	known
throw	threw	thrown
withdraw	withdrew	withdrawn

Miscellaneous

Simple Form	Simple Past	Past Participle
do	did	done
lie	lay	lain
swear	swore	sworn
tear	tore	torn
wear	wore	worn

Irregular Verbs

Group 7
Past tense and past participle the same

Simple Form	Simple Past	Past Participle	Simple Form	Simple Past	Past Participle
bend	bent	bent	mislay	mislaid	mislaid
bleed	bled	bled	pay	paid	paid
bring	brought	brought	read	read	read
build	built	built	say	said	said
burn	burnt	burnt	seek	sought	sought
buy	bought	bought	sell	sold	sold
catch	caught	caught	send	sent	sent
dig	dug	dug	shoot	shot	shot
feed	fed	fed	sit	sat	sat
feel	felt	felt	sleep	slept	slept
fight	fought	fought	slide	slid	slid
find	found	found	sneak	sneaked	sneaked
flee	fled	fled	speed	sped	sped
grind	ground	ground	spend	spent	spent
hang	hung	hung	spin	spun	spun
have	had	had	stand	stood	stood
hear	heard	heard	stick	stuck	stuck
hold	held	held	sting	stung	stung
keep	kept	kept	strike	struck	struck
lay	laid	laid	sweep	swept	swept
lead	led	led	swing	swung	swung
leave	left	left	teach	taught	taught
lend	lent	lent	tell	told	told
light	lit	lit	think	thought	thought
lose	lost	lost	understand	understood	understood
make	made	made	weep	wept	wept
mean	meant	meant	win	won	won
meet	met	met			

A booklet of tenses is available from Amazon.com and as an eBook. This booklet can be used for instant reference and is easily carried.

Unit 3

Adjectives

Structure Chart
Exercises
Writing Practice
References

Adjectives

Descriptive Adjectives

Descriptive adjectives tell the size, shape, age, color, origin, material, or give an opinion of a noun

Comparison

near careful	nearer more careful	not as near not as careful	less near less careful

Superlatives

easy important	easiest most important	least easy least important

Nouns as Adjectives

a *glass* vase
an *apple* pie
a *dishwasher*

Verbs as Adjectives

sleeping babies
an *interesting* story
dried flowers

Possessive Adjectives

It's *my* book	It's *her* book
It's *your* book	It's *our* book
It's *his* book	It's *their* book

Demonstrative Adjectives

This watch is expensive
That tree is blooming
These books are new
Those books are not for sale

Irregular Adjectives

bad	worse	worst
far (distance)	farther	farthest
far (depth)	further	furthest
good	better	best
little	less	least
many	more	most

Comparison Phrases

not as bad	slower than
not as far	more patient than
not as good	not as slow as
not as much	less expensive than
not as many	slower and slower
	more and more beautiful

More Comparisons

as pretty as almost as nearly as	similar to just as much more	different from not quite as very	better than like alike

*Use the given words to complete the sentences with **as...as**.*

1. a tornado and a hurricane

    _____ dangerous and wild as _____.

2. a lake and a pond

    _____ big as _____.

3. playing soccer and watching a soccer match

    In my opinion, _____ exciting as _____.

Complete the sentence with the correct comparative form.

4. There is a full moon tonight with not a cloud in the sky. Moonlight on the stream makes the water sparkle. Have you ever seen anything _____ than this?

Make positive sentences of comparison with the given nouns.

5. a pool/a puddle

    _____

6. a river/a brook

    _____

7. walking along a country lane/sitting in a garden on a quiet summer day

    _____

Make negative sentences of comparison with the given noun phrases

8. sitting in an easy chair/sitting on a park bench

    _____.

9. hiking along a path/climbing a mountain

    _____.

Complete the sentences using the words in the box.

| bright | hard | wet | happy |

10. Sunlight is much _____ than moonlight, even on an overcast day.

11. He used to be sad, but now he's a lot _____ than he used to be in the past.

12. As I continued walking home in miserable weather, it began to rain _____ and I got _____. By the time I got home, I was completely soaked.

Complete the sentences with superlative adjectives.

13. Costa Rica, in Central America, is one of _____ places in the world.

14. Everyone who played the game was exhausted, but I was _____ of all.

Use the phrases in the box to complete the sentences with superlatives.

| deep ocean | high mountains on earth | popular form of entertainment |

15. The Pacific is _____ in the world.

16. _____ are in the Himalayas.

17. One of _____ is the motion picture.

Complete the sentence using any appropriate form of the words in parentheses and adding any other words that are needed.

18. World Cup Soccer is *(big)* _____ sporting event in the world. It is viewed on TV by *(people)* _____ than any other event in sports.

Check your answers with the answer key on page 155

Choose a topic from the following list.
Choose the one that interests you the most.
Write about it.

free speech, illiteracy, racism, poverty, health, war, cultural differences

Use a variety of adjective forms from the structure chart on p. 16.
If you want to use more than one adjective to describe a noun,
refer to the Order of Adjectives chart on p. 20.

For editing services, email your writing as a WORD document to:
editessentials@aol.com

Adjective Order

Determiner	Observation	Physical Description				Origin	Material	Qualifier	Noun
		Size	Shape	Age	Color				
a	beautiful			old		Italian		touring	car
an	expensive			antique			silver		mirror
four	gorgeous		long-stemmed		red				roses
her			short		black				hair
our		big		old		English			sheepdog
those			square				wooden	hat	boxes
that	dilapidated	little						hunting	cabin
several		enormous		young		American		basketball	players
some	delicious					Thai			food

Unit 4

Adverbs

Structure Chart
Exercises
Writing Practice
References

Adverbs

Adverbs of Location
Placed after the verb

here	indoors
there	inside
everywhere	outdoors
nowhere	outside
not anywhere	upstairs
anywhere	downstairs
away	high
low	underneath

We looked for the book underneath the sofa.

Adverbs of Time
Placed after the verb

now	then
soon	early
later	late
afterwards	yet
already	recently
lately	still
not anymore	ago
today	tonight
yesterday	tomorrow

He didn't get an email yesterday.

Adverb & Noun Combinations as Adverbs of Time

the day before yesterday	this February	next week
the day after tomorrow	last night	the week after next
this morning	last week	next Friday
this afternoon	the week before last	next month
this evening	last Friday	next May
this week	last month	next spring
this Tuesday	last May	next year
this month	last year	sometime

They will visit us this month.   *It rained hard last Friday.*   *You should travel next week.*

Adverbs of Instance
Placed at the end of the phrase

once	three times
twice	ten times
again	a hundred times

He has called us at least ten times.

Adverbs of Frequency
Placed before the verb

never	sometimes
hardly ever	often
rarely	frequently
seldom	usually
occasionally	always

She seldom does her work on time.

Adverbs of Manner

quickly	more quickly	the most quickly
happily	more happily	the most happily
capably	more capably	the most capably
fast	faster	the fastest
well	better	the best
hard	harder	the hardest
late	later	the latest
early	earlier	the earliest

We worked quickly.   *We ran faster than you.*   *She did her work the best of all of us.*

Adverbs that Intensify Verbs, Adjectives & Other Adverbs

almost	fairly
nearly	pretty
hardly	rather
scarcely	quite
only	very
just	extremely
somewhat	unusually
really	too

We were almost ready at 6:00 am.   *I play tennis quite well.*

Rewrite the sentences to include the word in parentheses.

1. Carly doesn't play volleyball. *(often)*
   _____

2. He doesn't have to work late. *(usually)*
   _____

3. Josh is going to Spain. He is going to Portugal. *(also)*
   _____

4. Jane goes shopping on Saturday. *(frequently)*
   _____

Complete the sentences using the words in parentheses in the correct order.

5. I_____to bring my books to class. *(remember, never, can)*

6. I have seen them at baseball games, but I_____

   to them. *(never/have/spoken)*

7. If we hadn't taken the same class, we_____

   each other. *(never/met/would/have)*

*For each sentence, write a sentence with a similar meaning using **not...yet** + a verb from the list.*

   stop   finish   wake up   find   decide   leave

8. It's still snowing._____.

9. They're still repairing the roof. They_____.

10. The children are still sleeping._____.

11. Is Ann still looking for a new apartment?_____.

12. I'm still confused about what to do._____.

13. The plane is still waiting on the runway._____.

Replace the words in parentheses with an adverb.

14. I can't find my notebooks *(in any place)*_____.

15. I have searched for them *(in that place)*_____ and *(on the floor below)*_____. I have looked *(at a distance above)*_____ and *(a distance below)*_____. I have looked for them *(in all places)*_____.

16. We're going to celebrate *(the week after the present week)*_____.

17. I hope she passes the class *(a short time from now)* _____.

18. He doesn't visit his cousin. *(now, as before)*_____

Fill in the blanks with adverbs that intensify to complete the following ideas.

19. My air conditioner only cools the room to 79 degrees. It_____works.

20. My neighbor's air conditioner cools the room to 65 degrees. It_____works.

21. Another neighbor's air conditioner cools the room to 72 degrees. It_____ works.

22. The engineer is working on mine now. It is almost fixed. He says it_____ works.

Answer the questions making sure the adverbs are in the correct position.

23. Are they sleeping? *(still)*

    _____

24. Have you finished? *(already)*

    _____

25. How often does she practice? *(seldom)*

    _____

Check your answers with the answer key on p.age 155

Describe the characteristics and activities of a successful person.
Use adverbs to describe the actions this person might take.
How would you act in order to become successful?

*Use adverbs of manner, adverbs of frequency and adverbs
that intensify verbs, adjectives and other adverbs.
If you wish to use more than one adverb form to describe an action,
refer to the Order of Adverbs chart on p. 26.*

*For editing services, email your writing as a WORD document to:
editessentials@aol.com*

Adverb Order

Verb	Manner	Location	Frequency	Time	Purpose
Beth swims	enthusiastically	in the pool	every morning	before dawn	to keep in shape
Jeremy walks	impatiently	into town	every afternoon	before supper	to get a paper
Kathy naps	peacefully	in her room	every morning	before lunch	to get some rest

Fill in the blanks with your own sentences showing adverb order

Unit 5

Sentence Structure

Structure Chart
Exercises
Writing Practice
References

Sentence Structure

Simple Sentences

A simple sentence has one independent clause with a single subject and a single verb
We drove from Connecticut to Tennessee.

Compound Sentences

A compound sentence has more than one independent clause, joined with a coordinating conjunction
We were exhausted, but we arrived in time.

Complex Sentences

A complex sentence has one independent clause & one or more dependent clauses joined with a subordinating conjunction or a correlative conjunction
Although he arrived in time, he did not join in the activities.

Compound-Complex Sentences

A compound-complex sentence has one or more independent clauses & one or more dependent clauses joined with a subordinating or a correlative conjunction
After it was all over, he claimed that we were planning a surprise for him, although we think he really was surprised.

Run-On Sentences

A run-on sentence has two sentences joined without the correct punctuation
He arrived in time, he did not participate.
He arrived in time he did not participate.
Run-on sentences can be corrected by adding a coordinating conjunction, or by placing a period after the first independent clause and beginning the next independent clause with a capital letter. A semi-colon may also be used.

He arrived in time, but he did not participate.
He arrived in time. He did not participate.
He arrived in time; he did not participate.

Sentence Fragments

A sentence fragment is a dependent clause needing an independent clause to complete the thought

Though he arrived in time
(incomplete thought)

Complete the sentence with an independent clause

Though he arrived in time, he did not participate in the game.

Conjunctions

Coordinating Conjunctions	Subordinating Conjunctions		Correlative Conjunctions
and	before	after	both...and
but	until	when	not only...but also
or	while	so that	either...or
yet	if	unless	neither...nor
for	where	as if	whether...or not
nor	rather than	that	
so			

Combine the following sentences by using the conjunctions in parentheses.

1. Tara went to see a movie. She went to dinner afterwards with her friends.

    (not only...but also)

    _____

    _____

2. She tried to pass the test. She failed. *(yet)*

    _____

3. Tara didn't go to see a movie. Her boyfriend didn't go either.

    (neither...nor)

    _____

    _____

Correct these run-on sentences.

4. The reports were all mixed up on the desk, therefore, we couldn't find the right report when we needed it.

    _____

5. I have an idea that we should consider it might help us solve our problems.

    _____

6. The icicles were melting, the brass bucket caught the freezing drops of water.

    _____

Indicate whether the following phrases are complete sentences or fragments.

7. While it was raining yesterday, and there was a flood on the road.

    (a) complete sentence
    (b) fragment

8. Until I can manage to wake up earlier, I will tend to always be late.

    (a) complete sentence
    (b) fragment

9. Maybe I will see a movie instead before I go shopping at the mall.

    (a) complete sentence
    (b) fragment

For each sentence, choose the option that corrects the sentence.

10. Right after summer vacation and at the very beginning of academic classes in August

    (a) This sentence is correct
    (b) Fragment: put a comma after *August* and finish the sentence
    (b) Run-on: put a comma after *vacation*

11. Confused by the unemployment rate and alarmed by the fact that construction projects were canceled

    (a) There is nothing wrong with this sentence.
    (b) Run-on: put a comma after *unemployment*
    (c) Fragment: put a comma after *canceled* and finish the sentence

12. We have to rewrite all these reports, straighten the furniture, clean the desks, stack the books on the shelf, and clean up the mess on the floor; tell someone about the broken window, the malfunctioning thermostat; and the desk that doesn't belong to anyone

    (a) There is nothing wrong with this sentence.
    (b) Run-on: the sentence should be broken into three smaller sentences
    (c) Fragment: although the sentence is very long, it's missing a verb string
    (d) Run-on: change the two semicolons to commas

Select the sentence that is NOT a sentence fragment.

13. (a) Carol visiting her new college in Hawaii.
    (b) Taking a test during the semester
    (c) Finding a four-leaf clover in the meadow is not easy
    (d) Her efforts, while wonderful, not sufficient

Check your answers with the answer key on page 155

Think of small moments in your life that had meaning for you.
Choose one of them and write about it.

Use a variety of sentence structures to write your paragraph.
Check the basic sentence structures on the structure chart on p. 28
and the more detailed sentence structures on the reference chart on pp. 32 - 33.

For editing services, email your writing as a WORD document to:
editessentials@aol.com

Variety in Sentence Structure

Expanded Subjects
This sentence describes the subject noun

That boy over there, *the one in the green shirt,* is my sister's friend.

Expanded Verbs
This sentence describes the verb

The class read the story, *without interest at first, and then with increasing concentration.*

Expanded Object
This sentence describes the object noun

We watched the tennis star, *athletic and strong*, winning his tenth championship match.

Loose Sentences

This sentence is a basic statement with a string of details added to it.

Bells rang. *(basic sentence)*
Bells rang, *filling the air with their noisy clanging, startling birds from their roosts, bringing people into the streets to hear the news.*

Periodic Sentences

In this sentence, additional details are placed before the basic statement.

John gave his mother flowers. *(basic sentence)*
John, *usually the tough one, the normally sullen boy, who refused to show any feelings,* gave his mother flowers.

Interrupted Periodic Sentence

In this sentence, additional details are added inside the basic statement.

Love is blind. *(basic sentence)*
Love, *as everyone knows except those who happen to be in love*, is blind.

Cumulative Sentence

In this sentence, additional details are added before and after the basic statement.

(basic sentence)
John was angry.
(periodic statement)
John was suddenly, violently angry.
(more periodic)
John, usually a very calm man, was suddenly, violently angry.
(ending detail)
John, usually a very calm man, was suddenly, violently angry, so angry that he lost complete control.
(beginning detail)
Usually a very calm man, John was suddenly, violently angry, so angry that he lost complete control of his feelings.

Cumulative Sentence

The roof tile fell.

The roof tile suddenly fell.

After one hundred years, the roof tile suddenly and without warning, fell in the night.

After one hundred years, buffeted by wind and rain, the roof tile suddenly and without warning fell in the night.

After one hundred long years, constantly buffeted by fierce wind and rain, the loose roof tile fell suddenly and without warning onto the street in the night.

After one hundred long years, constantly buffeted by fierce wind and icy rain, the ancient roof tile, which had been loose for decades, fell suddenly and without warning onto the street in the night and into the path of a young girl.

After one hundred long, lonely years, constantly buffeted by fierce wind and icy rain, the ancient and historic roof tile, which had been loose for decades, fell suddenly and without warning onto the quiet and deserted street in the still night, and into the path of an unsuspecting young girl.

After one hundred long, lonely, forgotten years, constantly buffeted by fierce wind and icy rain, the ancient and historic roof tile, which had been loose for decades, fell suddenly, silently and without warning onto the quiet and deserted street in the still night, and into the path of an unsuspecting young girl, who picked it up and took it home.

After one hundred long, lonely, forgotten years, constantly buffeted by fierce wind and icy rain, the ancient and historic roof tile, which had been loose for decades and threatening to fall, fell suddenly, silently and without warning, onto the quiet and deserted street in the still and motionless night, and into the path of an unsuspecting young girl, who picked it up and took it home to give to her mother as a gift, who treasured it and placed it on the old mantel.

A spiral-bound book,
English Sentence Patterns*,*
gives more detailed practice.
It is available from Amazon.com and as an eBook.

The book includes *simple, compound, complex* and *compound-complex* sentences with *adjective* and *adverb* modifiers, *prepositional phrase* modifers and *present & past participial phrase* modifiers.

Adjective Modifiers

Spring flowers are blooming.

Adverb Modifiers

Spring flowers are blooming freely.

Prepositional Phrase Modifiers

Spring flowers in the garden bloom freely by the gate.

Present Participial Phrase Modifiers

Spring flowers, growing this year, bloom freely in the garden.

Past Participial Phrase Modifiers

Spring flowers, planted last autumn, bloom freely in the garden.

Transitions

**Structure Chart
Exercises
Writing Practice
References**

Transitions

Expressing Chronological Order

first	in the first place
second	next
then	after that
meanwhile	in the meantime
finally	subsequently

In the meantime, **she had read the book,** *so she* **subsequently** *gave it to her brother.*

Making an Argument more Convincing

and	also
as well as	in addition
plus	besides
furthermore	on top of that
to top it all off	moreover

Furthermore, once she had read the book, she gave it to her brother.

Illustrating Previous Information

in fact	as a matter of fact
indeed	actually

As a matter of fact, she gave the book to her brother.

Correcting Previous Information

as a matter of fact	in fact
actually	

In fact, she actually gave the book to her brother, not her sister.

Contradicting Previous Information

but	however
on the other hand	in contrast
nevertheless	still
yet	instead
otherwise	

Otherwise, she would have given the book to her friend instead.

Explaining Previous Information

in other words	that is
I mean	for example
for instance	specifically

She gave the book to her brother specifically, for example, and not to her friend.

Reducing the Importance of Previous Information

anyway	anyhow
at any rate	in any case

Her friend had already read the book anyway.

Verifying Previous Information

really	indeed
naturally	of course
certainly	

Of course, her brother really enjoyed reading the book.

Indicating the Consequences of an Action

so	consequently
therefore	thus
as a result	

As a result everyone in the group read the book.

Expressing Reasons for an Action

because	since

Since the book was very interesting, everyone read it in one week.

Expressing Concession or Condition

although	even though
in spite of the fact that	
even if	

Even if the book had not been interesting, everyone would have read it.

Summarizing

so	in the end
in short	in summary
in conclusion	ultimately

Ultimately, everyone enjoyed reading the book.

Identify the transitions by their function.

1. *In the first place,* I gave a party for my sister's birthday.

    (a) making an argument more convincing
    (b) expressing chronological order
    (c) illustrating previous information

2. He is hard-working and intelligent *as well as* responsible.

    (a) contradicting previous information
    (b) correcting previous information
    (c) making an argument more convincing

3. I know New York very well. *As a matter of fact,* I lived there for many years.

    (a) illustrating previous information
    (b) reducing the importance of previous information
    (c) correcting previous information

4. He's very intelligent; *on the other hand*, he tends to be somewhat irresponsible.

    (a) verifying previous information
    (b) explaining previous information
    (c) contradicting previous information

5. He didn't study architecture. *As a matter of fact,* he studied engineering.

    (a) correcting previous information
    (b) indicating the consequences of an action
    (c) explaining previous information

6. When we arrived at Mia's house, she wasn't there. *Consequently,* we couldn't ask her to come to the mall with us.

    (a) reducing the importance of previous information
    (b) expressing chronological order
    (c) indicating the consequences of an action

7. I think we should examine other programs. *In other words*, I think this one is unworkable.

    (a) explaining previous information
    (b) verifying previous information
    (c) expressing reasons for an action

8. I don't really want to take the job, but I'm sending them my resumé *anyway*.

    (a) expressing concession or condition
    (b) summarizing
    (c) reducing the importance of the previous information

9. *Naturally*, every student is happy that this day has arrived at long last.

    (a) verifying previous information
    (b) correcting previous information
    (c) expressing concession or condition

10. *Since* she invited you, it is important that you tell her whether you are going to the dinner or not.

    (a) making an argument more convincing
    (b) illustrating previous information
    (c) expressing reasons for an action

11. *Even if* the weather is beautiful, we are not going out for a walk.

    (a) expressing concession or condition
    (b) summarizing
    (c) contradicting previous information

12. *Although* the weather was warm, the children did not want to play outside.

    (a) indicating the consequences of an action
    (b) verifying previous information
    (c) expressing concession or condition

13. *In conclusion* I would like to thank all of you who have come here today to listen to our newest sales concepts.

    (a) summarizing
    (b) reducing the importance of previous information
    (c) illustrating previous information

Use any of the transition forms to create original sentences.

1. _____

2. _____

3. _____

Check your answers with the answer key on page 155

Imagine yourself descending a staircase into your past.
What do you recall?
Write about the earliest memory that comes to your mind.

Use transitions from the structure chart on p. 36 to link your ideas and to make them clear.
Check the reference chart on p.40 for additional connecting words.

For editing services, email your writing as a WORD document to:
editessentials@aol.com

Transitions in Essays

Narrative Essays

after	as	as soon as
before	by the time	earlier
now	at first	first, second
immediately	later	later on
meanwhile	next	finally
suddenly	then	until
when	eventually	soon
at the same time		by this time
two hours later		by the time

Descriptive Essays

above	between	in back of
nearby	on one side	over
behind	beyond	in front of
next to	on the other side	below
in	inside	on
outside	the most important	
	the least important	

Comparison & Contrast Essays

although	however	like
unlike	but	in comparison
likewise	similarly	whereas
even though	in contrast	nevertheless
though	instead	one similarity
on the other hand		on the contrary
another similarity		on the one hand
one difference		

Persuasive Essays

accordingly	because	despite
in summary	admittedly	but
even so	in addition	after all
certainly	even though	although
moreover	in conclusion	finally
consequently	finally	in fact
meanwhile	for this reason	since

Definition Essays

also	in particular	for example
like	another way	in addition
one way	specifically	
	one characteristic	

Exemplification Essays

for example	moreover	besides
for instance	finally	first
furthermore	specifically	also
the next example	in addition	
another example	one example	
the most important example		

Cause & Effect Essays

accordingly	as a result
for	since
the first effect	because
another cause	so
for this reason	therefore
the first reason	moreover
another effect	
consequently	
the first cause	
the most important effect	
the most important cause	

Classfication Essays

one kind
the first category
one way
another kind
the last group
another way
the final type
the next part
the first group
the most important group
the least important group

Process Essays

after that	first
at the same time	next
subsequently	before
the last step	now
after this	when
at this point	as
immediately	during
the first step	later
the final step	once
the next step	while
as soon as	finally
meanwhile	soon
at the end	then

Unit 7

Modifiers

**Structure Chart
Exercises
Writing Practice
References**

Modifiers

Modifiers are words, phrases or clauses that provide description in sentences

Types of Modifiers

Appositive Phrases
This phrase modifies a noun

The clamor of the bells, *a solemn sound in the night,* wakened the town at dawn.

Participial Phrases
This phrase modifies a verb

The bells rang, *filling the quiet night* with sonorous clanging.

Infinitive Phrases
This phrase indicates a purpose

The bells rang *to send their loud message* through the sleeping town.

Prepositional Phrases
This phrase indicates a location

The bells *in the ancient steeple* rang at midnight on the last day of the festival.

Adjectives
This phrase describes a noun directly

The *joyous, celebratory* bells rang at midnight on the day of the festival.

Adverbs
This phrase describes a verb directly

The bells rang, *loudly and joyously,* through the night on market day.

Errors with Modifiers

Modifiers need to be near the word being described

Dangling Modifiers

Dependent on the weather, it is natural to wish for the sun to appear.
Because we are dependent on the weather, it is natural for us to wish for the sun to appear.

Misplaced Modifiers

The other day, I rode an elephant *in my pajamas.*
The other day, *in my pajamas,* I rode an elephant.

Squinting Modifiers

Defining your terms clearly strengthens your argument.
If you define your terms clearly, your argument will be strengthened.

clearly strengthens your argument.
If you define your terms, you are clearly strengthening your argument.

Split Infinitives

Infinitives are never separated.

The marketing team voted *to*, before the launch, *run* an ad campaign. *(incorrect)*

The marketing team voted *to run* an ad campaign before the launch. *(incorrect)*

Misplaced Words

Be careful with *almost, hardly, nearly, just, only, merely*

I *nearly* earned $3000 *(I was in the position of possibly earning $3000)*
I earned *nearly* $3000 *(I earned almost $3000)*

Rewrite the following sentences, which contain dangling and misplaced modifiers, so that each modifier refers to a word or word group it can logically modify.

1. Sweating in the humid sunshine, the tennis balls were bounced back and forth across the tennis court by the players.

2. Exhausted after the long day at work, our time was finally spent relaxing.

3. Made by my niece, the flowers in the vase brightened the room.

4. The book kept me awake all night that I borrowed from you last week.

5. A small reflecting pool surrounded the ancient temple filled with goldfish.

6. Becoming starkly colder, snow began to fall heavily.

7. Though only the age of ten, the modeling agency awarded her the contract.

8. Green, slimy amphibians with bulbous noses, science students find frogs extremely interesting.

9. With the sound of thunder and splashing of water, I witnessed a tsunami hitting the shore.

10. Going further westward, the scenery became more and more beautiful.

11. Although totally exhausted, the party was so good that we stayed all night.

    _____

12. Angrily blowing from north to south, we were snowed in by a terrible blizzard last weekend.

    _____

Select the correctly written sentence in these groups.

13. (a) I like to walk along the beach doing exercises.
    (b) I like to walk along the beach while doing exercises.

14. (a) The soccer team only won four games this year.
    (b) The soccer team won only four games this year.

15. (a) With nothing to do for the weekend, we decided to see a movie.
    (b) With nothing to do for the weekend, a movie seemed a good idea.

16. (a) The audience was enchanted by the monkeys swinging wildly through the trees.
    (b) Swinging wildly through the trees, the audience was enchanted by the monkeys.

Which of the following sentences contains a dangling modifier?

17. (a) To raise a child, patience is needed.
    (b) Moving slowly, we finally reached the river.
    (c) After eating lunch on the beach, we took a short nap.
    (d) all of the above
    (e) none of the above

Which of the following sentences contains a dangling participial phrase?

18. (a) Charles regretted missing the giant sale last month.
    (b) To complete the grammar quiz on time, you will have to work fast.
    (c) When taking a grammar test, concentration is necessary.
    (d) all of the above
    (e) none of the above

Which of the following sentences contains a dangling gerund phrase?

19. (a) On completing the assignment, leaving the room is acceptable.
    (b) Wearing a helmet is an excellent safety precaution.
    (c) When she talks to her friends, she realizes that she is very fortunate.
    (e) all of the above

Check your answers with the answer key on page 155

Think of a realization that changed your life
or that could have changed your life.
Write about it.

*Use modifiers from the structure chart on p. 42 to describe your ideas.
Study the reference chart on p. 45 for additional uses.*

*For editing services, email your writing as a WORD document to:
editessentials@aol.com*

Modifiers in Motion

Multiple Modifiers

Poor Stephen, who just wanted a quick nap on the sofa to refresh himself, qietly lay down, yawning with fatigue, as a soft breeze created a gentle feeling conducive to a very long and refreshing sleep.

Adjective
poor

Adjective Clause
who just wanted a quick nap

Prepositional Phrase
on the sofa

Infinitive Phrase
to refresh himself

Adverb Phrase
quietly lay down

Participial Phrase
yawning with fatigue

Adverb Clause
as a soft breeze created a gentle feeling

Appositive Phrase
conducive to a very long and refreshing sleep

Amusing Errors

The tall boy drove the car to lead the parade with red hair.

My brother just watches one TV channel.

After singing a solo on stage, the captive audience applauded her performance.

While taking a nap, the volcano erupted.

The new student will sit in the corner seat wearing a red shirt.

With a hope that the weather would improve, the corn was planted in the afternoon.

Completely destroyed by the freak tornado, he had to rebuild his damaged barn.

While standing in line at the theater, thunder could be heard.

Unit 8

Gerunds & Infinitives

Structure Chart
Exercises
Writing Practice
References

Gerunds & Infinitives

Gerunds as Subjects

The gerund form (*present participle with ing*) can be used as the subject of a sentence

Playing tennis is fun.

Gerunds as Objects

The gerund form (*present participle with ing*) can be used as the object of a sentence

We enjoy *playing* tennis.

Gerunds as Objects of Prepositions

The gerund form (*present participle with ing*) can be used as the object of a preposition

He's excited about *playing* tennis.

Verbs followed by Gerunds

He *avoided* answering the question.
I will *consider* going with you.
They *discussed* opening a new business.
He *quit* trying to solve the problem.
I *remember* meeting him last year.
She *suggested* swimming in the neighbor's pool.
She *stopped* attending class last week.

Verbs followed by Infinitives

I can't *afford* to buy the house.
They *agreed* to help us.
They *arranged* to meet at the airport.
He *continued* to speak.
I *decided* to leave on Monday.
I *demand* to know who is responsible.
She *deserves* to win the prize.
I *expect* to enter graduate school in the fall.

Verbs followed by Gerunds or Infinitives

He began to walk slowly.
He began walking slowly.
She continued to write.
She continued writing.
They learned to drive.
They learned driving.
We like to shop.
We like shopping.
You prefer to study.
You prefer studying.
We started to run.
We started running.
I can't afford to fly.
I can't afford flying.

Prepositional Expressions Followed by Gerunds

be accused of	blame for	forgive for	prevent from
be accustomed to	be capable of	be guilty of	be scared of
in addition to	be committed to	instead of	stop from
be afraid of	complain about	be interested in	succeed in
apologize for	dream of	look forward to	take advantage of
believe in	be excited about	be opposed to	think of

Adjectives Followed by Infinitives

glad	sorry	ashamed	determined	surprised
pleased	sad	ready	careful	amazed
delighted	upset	prepared	reluctant	astonished
content	disappointed	anxious	afraid	shocked
relieved	embarrassed	eager	certain	stunned
lucky	proud	willing	likely	motivated

Insert the correct form, either a gerund or an infinitive.

1. I need *(take)* _____ a break because I'm getting very tired.

2. Sometimes drivers avoid *(look)* _____ at the yellow light if they don't want *(stop)* _____ and wait for the green light.

3. The beauty salon refused *(take)* _____ a check, accepting only credit cards.

4. Keep *(walk)* _____. You're almost there.

5. Don't forget *(ask)* _____ Jane *(call)* _____ me about *(go)* _____ *(dance)* _____ tomorrow.

6. Sally reminded me *(ask)* _____ you *(tell)* _____ Bob *(remember)* _____ *(bring)* _____ his soccer ball to the picnic.

Complete the sentences with appropriate gerunds.

7. We had a lot of fun _____ games and _____ at the picnic.

8. Richard is sitting in class _____ notes for the next exam.

9. He has a hard time _____ up his mind about anything to do with health.

10. Dorothy was lying under a tree _____ to the birds in the branches.

11. I noticed the children _____ in the muddy yard.

Check all the correct answers.

12. (a) We hope seeing them soon.
    (b) We hope to see them soon.
    (c) We hope you to see them soon.

13. (a) We asked you to call us.
    (b) We asked to call us.
    (c) We asked calling us.

14. (a) I invited to go to the park with the group.
    (b) I invited Ella to go to the park with the group.
    (c) Ella was invited to go to the park with the group.

Complete the phrases with your own words, using gerunds.

15. Every evening I spend at least an hour_____.

16. In my free time, I have fun_____ and_____.

17. Sometimes I waste money_____ or_____.

18. I think it's fun to spend all day_____ in addition to_____.

19. Sometimes I have trouble_____ as well as_____.

Complete the sentences with an appropriate gerund or infinitive.

20. We're going to Spain this summer. Would you like_____ with us?

21. I had lost my wallet, so Jenny offered_____ me a little money.

22. Would you mind_____ the ladder for me?

23. Lori pretended_____ the last question.

24. Mrs. Jackson warned her young son not_____ the cake before the party.

25. Residents are not allowed_____ any pets in the apartment building.

26. All applicants are required_____ a placement examination.

27. My boss expects me_____ the work immediately.

28. Joan and David were considering_____ married in June, but they finally decided_____ until August, when the weather is better.

29. When we were in New York, we had a really good time_____ in Central Park on sunny days.

Which pairs have basically the same meaning? Which have different meanings? Circle S or D.

30. (a) It began to snow.   S D
      It began snowing.

   (c) He forgot to buy the gift.   S D
      He forgot buying a gift.

   (b) I stopped to talk to him.   S D
      I stopped talking to him.

   (d) We like to listen to music.   S D
      We like listening to music.

Check your answers with the answer key on page 155

Think about what needs to be done in the following situation.
Make a list and write about the items on your list.
a person going to another country for a month

*Use gerund clauses and infinitive clauses on the structure chart on p. 48
to write your paragraph.
Refer to the additional forms on the reference chart on p. 52.*

*For editing services, email your writing as a WORD document to:
editessentials@aol.com*

Gerunds & Infinitives

Verbs followed by Gerunds

admit	advise	anticipate
appreciate	avoid	can't bear
begin	complete	consider
continue	delay	deny
discuss	dislike	enjoy
finish	forget	hate
can't help	keep	like
love	mention	mind
miss	postpone	practice
prefer	quit	recall
recollect	recommend	regret
remember	resent	resist
risk	can't stand	start
stop	suggest	tolerate
try	understand	keep

Verbs followed by Infinitives

afford	agree	appear
arrange	ask	can't bear
beg	begin	care
claim	consent	continue
decide	demand	deserve
expect	fail	forget
hate	hesitate	hope
intend	learn	need
want	refuse	ask
go	pretend	allow

Verbs followed by a Noun or Pronoun + Infinitive

advise the child	allow them	ask us
beg the boss	cause it	dare him
challenge us	convince her	forbid us
encourage us	force them	invite him
expect the company	instruct us	order her
hire the man	permit her	need it
persuade the boss	remind us	require us
teach the children	tell them	urge them
warn the group	want it	tell him

Special Expressions followed by Gerunds

We had fun We had a good time	*playing* tennis.
I had trouble I had difficulty I had a hard time I had a difficult time	*finding* the house.
Sam spends time He wastes time	*studying*.
She sat at her desk I stood in the room He lay in bed	*writing*. *wondering*. *reading*.
I found George I saw her	*using* my phone. *sitting* at my desk.

Verbs + Gerunds or Infinitives with no Difference in Meaning

It began *to rain*. It began *raining*.
I started *to work*. I started *working*.
It continued *to snow*. It continued *snowing*.
He likes *to dance*. He likes *dancing*.
She prefers *to read*. She prefers *reading*.

Verbs + Gerunds or Infinitives with a Difference in Meaning

They stopped *talking/to talk*.
He remembered *to close/closing* the door.
She forgot *to return/returning* the book.

GO + Gerund

go biking go boating go bowling	go canoeing go dancing go fishing	go jogging go climbing go running	go shopping go skating go skiing	go sledding go swimming go camping	go hiking go sailing go diving

Unit 9

Prepositions

Structure Chart
Exercises
Writing Practice
References

Preposition Combinations

Preposition + Noun Combinations

in English in good shape in a book	in the rain in a hurry in a low voice	in a good mood in charge in a suit	in style in a car in good health
on a bus on television	on a bicycle on paper	on foot on a nice day	on fire on strike
at home	at school	at work	at the airport
by chance	by accident	with luck	with time

Preposition + Adjective Combinations

absent from accustomed to acquainted with addicted to afraid of amazed at amazed by amused at amused by angry at angry about annoyed at annoyed by annoyed with anxious about ashamed of associated with aware of bad for bad to bewildered by bored by capable of careless with clear to cluttered with committed to compared to composed of concerned about confused by connected to consist of content with convinced of coordinated with	courteous to crazy about crowded with dedicated to dependent on devoted to different from difficult for disappointed in disappointed with disgusted by divorced from dressed in eager for easy for embarrassed by engaged to envious of equal to equipped with excited about exhausted from exposed to faithful to familiar with fascinated by filled with finished by finished with fond of friendly to friendly with frightened of frustrated by full of furnished with	gone from good at good for good to good with grateful for grateful to guilty of happy about happy for happy with hard for honest about honest with hungry for inferior to innocent of interested in invited to involved in involved with irritated by jealous of kind of kind to known by known for made at made by made for made of made with married to nervous about nice to opposed to	patient with pleased with polite to prepared by prepared for prepared with proud of protected from qualified for ready for related to remembered for responsible for responsible to rid of sad about safe from satisfied with scared of shocked by similar to sorry about sorry for suitable for superior to sure of surprised at surprised by terrified by terrified of tired of thirsty for upset by upset with worried about worried by

Preposition Combinations

Preposition + Verb Combinations

accuse of	complain about	graduate from	rely on
add to	complain to	help with	rescue from
admit to	concentrate on	hear from	respond to
agree with	consist of	hide from	rest from
apologize for	contribute to	hope for	separate from
apologize to	count on	insist on	stare at
apply to	cover with	know about	stop from
approve of	decide on	laugh about	subscribe to
argue about	depend on	laugh at	substitute for
argue with	disagree with	laugh with	subtract from
arrive at	discuss with	lend to	succeed at
arrive in	dream about	listen to	succeed in
ask about	dream of	look forward to	take advantage of
believe in	distinguish from	object to	take care of
belong to	excuse for	participate in	talk about
belong with	excuse from	pay for	talk to
blame for	escape from	plan on	tell about
borrow from	escape to	prevent from	thank for
complain about	excel in	prohbiit from	think about
care for	fight for	protect from	warn about
compare to	forget about	provide with	wonder about
compare with	forgive for	recover from	worry about

Prepositional Phrases

Prepositional phrases are parts of English sentences
that begin with a preposition and are followed by a noun.
A sentence may contain several prepositional phrases.
Adjectives may describe the nouns in the prepositional phrases
and in the rest of the sentence.
Adverbs may describe the verbs in the prepositional phrases
and in the rest of the sentence.

The students *in the library* were preparing *for the test*.
We enjoyed the party *at your house on Saturday afternoon*.
The children went *to the zoo with their family on the weekend*.

The visiting students *in the newly-built library* were eagerly preparing *for the final test*.
We thoroughly enjoyed the elegant party *at your beautiful home on Saturday in the late afternoon*.
The boisterous children went happily *to the old city zoo with their willing family the past weekend*.

Complete the sentences with the correct prepositions.

1. Tom has always been devoted_____his family.
2. I'm afraid I don't agree_____you at all this time.
3. I wasn't aware_____the problem or I would have helped.
4. I'm excited_____the concert, the first one this year.
5. The solution is clear_____me and it should be_____you also.
6. Protect your eyes_____the sun at all times.
7. Mr. Porter is nice_____everyone except the driver of the van.
8. I'm thirsty_____a big glass of water after that long walk.
9. I'm not familiar_____that book at all, even though I've seen it before.
10. Anna is very happy_____getting a new job in that fantastic company.
11. Could you please help me_____these two heavy suitcases?
12. Who was responsible_____the accident on the corner this morning?
13. My courses are similar_____yours, but different_____Ben's.
14. I'm crazy_____quilting. I'm very interested_____it.
15. Joan graduated_____high school two years ago with high grades.
16. I arrived_____this city last month on an overnight shuttle bus.
17. I arrived_____the airport around eight, after a very long trip.
18. I complained_____the landlord_____the dark hallway.
19. Carlos was absent_____class six times last term and may not pass.
20. Fruit consists mostly_____water and sugar.
21. Some children are very polite_____adults, but they argue_____their friends all the time.
22. I'm not ready_____my trip because I haven't packed everything yet.

23. Are you familiar _____ ancient Greek or Roman history?

24. I admire you _____ your ability to laugh _____ yourself all the time.

25. Are you arguing _____ each other again _____ your future?

26. The city was warned in advance _____ the hurricane that came last weekend.

27. I apologized _____ Ann _____ stepping on her toe again.

28. Please forgive me _____ forgetting your birthday once more.

29. Children always depend _____ their parents for love and support.

30. I compared the parks in this city _____ those in my hometown.

31. Umbrellas protect us _____ the rain and occasionally from the sun.

32. We're relying _____ him to help us move to our new house.

33. My boss reluctantly excused me _____ the meeting last week.

34. I'm trying to concentrate _____ this problem at the present moment.

35. Did you tell your parents _____ the dent in their new car yet?

36. We're hoping _____ good weather tomorrow so that we can go sailing.

37. I'm not at all accustomed _____ cold weather.

38. He insisted _____ knowing the truth and deciding what to do about it.

39. George wondered _____ his team's chances of winning the tennis tournament.

40. I don't approve _____ his choice of study but it's his decision.

41. The official warned us _____ the danger of traveling there without a guide.

42. Does it matter _____ you what time I call you this evening?

43. What's the matter _____ you today? You're so gloomy.

Check your answers with the answer key on page 155

Think of the events that have shaped your life.
Make a list and choose one.
Write about it..

Use prepositional phrases with nouns, adjectives, verbs and adverbs from the structure chart on pp. 54 - 55 to write your paragraph. For prepositions of place, direction, time, and other relationships, study the reference chart on p. 59.

For editing services, email your writing as a WORD document to: editessentials@aol.com

Prepositions

Prepositions that Indicate Place

over above below beneath under underneath	behind in back of in front of ahead of across from opposite	against by beside next to between among	near close to far from beyond on upon	off in inside within out of outside of

in	*on*	*at*	*in*
a continent a country a state a city	a coast a beach a side a street a floor	a building the market my house home an address	a specific place the office the kitchen the corner

Prepositions that Indicate Direction

across along by past	through around down up	to toward from back to	into out of onto off

Prepositions that Indicate Time

before after during	since until up to	around about by	for through while

in	*on*	*at*	*in time*	*at present/at this moment*
a century a decade a year a season a month a time of day	a day a date a holiday certain days	night a specific time	not too late *on time* at the expected time	now

Prepositions that Indicate Other Relationships

by	by email, by car, by the boss, by hand
with	with friends, with a sewing machine
in	in watercolor, in oils, in wood, in metal
of	silk, cotton, silver, gold

from	from my niece, from Paris
instead of	I'll take tea instead of coffee
except	I want all the shirts except the pink one
as	He was known as a great leader.

Sentence Patterns with Prepositional Phrases

At a sufficient distance over the woods,
the sound of the bells acquires a hum,
as if the pine needles were the strings of a harp.

This is a delicious evening,
when the whole mind is one sense,
drinking delight
through every pore.

I have occasional visits
in the long winter evenings,
when the snow falls fast
and the wind howls in the woods.

The frogs croak to usher in the night,
and the note of the whippoorwill
is borne on the rippling wind
from over the water.

On warm evenings,
I frequently sat in my boat
playing the flute,
and saw the moon traveling
over the water.

The rain was now over,
and a rainbow above the eastern woods
promised a fair evening,
so I set out on my journey gladly
and with anticipation.

My house was on the side of a hill,
on the edge of the large wood,
in the middle of a young forest of pines,
near the pond,
to which a narrow path led down the hill.

Here comes the cattle train
bearing cattle of a thousand hills,
whirled along like leaves
blown from the mountains
by the September gales.

Selected from
Walden
Henry David Thoreau

Unit 10

Phrasal Verbs

Structure Chart
Exercises
Writing Practice
References

Phrasal Verbs

Phrasal verbs are two and three word verb + preposition combinations that have special meanings not related to the actual words used. They are a form of idiomatic English which must be learned through practice.

Separable Phrasal Verbs

ask out	ask for a date
call back	return a phone call
call off	cancel
call up	make a phone call
cross out	draw a line through
figure out	find the solution
fill in	complete a blank space
fill out	write information on a form
fill up	fill completely with a liquid
find out	discover information
give back	return something
hand in	give homework to teacher
hand out	give something to everyone
hang up	hang on a hanger or hook
have on	wear
look over	examine carefully
look up	look for information
make up	invent
pay back	return borrowed money
pick up	lift
point out	call attention to
print out	create a paper copy
put away	put in its proper place
put back	return to original place
put down	stop holding
put off	postpone
put on	place clothes on one's body
put out	extinguish a flame
shut off	stop a machine or light
take off	remove clothes from body
tear down	destroy a building
tear out	remove from a book by tearing
tear up	tear into small pieces
throw away	discard
throw out	discard
try on	put on clothing to check fit
turn around	change to opposite direction
turn back	change to opposite direction
turn down	decrease the volume
turn off	stop a machine or light
turn on	start a machine or light
turn over	turn the top side to the bottom
turn up	increase the volume
wake up	stop sleeping
write down	write a note on paper

Some phrasal verbs can place the object between the verb and the preposition

blow out	extinguish a flame
bring back	return
bring up	mention
cheer up	make happier
clean up	make neat
give away	get rid of by giving
help out	assist
lay off	stop employment
leave on	not turn off or remove
take back	return
take out	invite out and pay
talk over	discuss
think over	consider
work out	solve

Non-Separable Phrasal Verbs

call on	ask someone to speak
come from	originate
get in	enter a vehicle
get off	leave a vehicle
get on	enter a vehicle
get out of	leave
get over	recover from illness/shock
look into	investigate
run into	meet by chance

Three Word Phrasal Verbs

carry on with	go over to
come along with	grow up in
come over to	hang out with
cut out of	hang around with
drop in on	look out for
find out about	keep away from
fool around with	run away with
get along with	run out of
get back from	set out for
get through with	sign up for
get together with	sit around with
go back to	watch out for

Phrasal Verbs

Intransitive Phrasal Verbs

Intransitive phrasal verbs are not followed by an object

break down	stop functioning properly	*hang up*	end a phone conversation
break out	happen suddenly	*move in*	start living in a new house
break up	end a relationship	*move out*	stop living in a place
come in	enter a room or building	*show up*	come, appear
dress up	put on nice clothes	*sit back*	lean against a chair back
eat out	eat in a restaurant	*sit down*	go from standing to sitting
fall down	fall to the ground	*speak up*	speak louder
get up	get out of bed in the morning	*stand up*	go from sitting to standing
give up	quit trying	*start over*	begin again
go on	continue	*stay up*	not go to bed
go out	not stay home	*take off*	go up in an airplane
grow up	become an adult		

Sentence Samples with Phrasal Verbs

We had a serious argument, but with time, our disagreement will *blow over*.

With a lot of effort, he will *bring about* the success of his company.

Let's *close up* our work for today and go home!

He had promised to help us but he did not *come through* in time.

Our contract with the distributor will not succeed; it will *fall through* next week.

The business is having great economic difficulty and we don't know how we will *get through* it.

After a whole day trying to finish the report, the people involved finally *gave up*.

Please *look through* the completed business plan and let us know if we should make any changes.

Complete the sentences with appropriate phrasal verbs.

1. If it's cold outside, you should not go out without_____a coat.

2. I took my book from him and_____where I had found it.

3. If I don't want to work, I watch TV,_____doing my homework.

4. Often students_____their homework_____to a later time.

5. A sudden noise _____ the children _____ at midnight.

6. It was dark when I got home last night, so I_____the lights_____.

7. When I raised my hand in class, the teacher never_____me.

8. While I was shopping in the mall last week, I_____an old friend.

9. Sam finally feels all right again because he_____his cold.

10. I made sure to_____my gloves before planting the flowers.

11. Stacy needed to find some important information so she_____the information on her laptop and _____ it_____ in her notebook.

12. I tried to solve the math problem, but I couldn't_____it_____.

13. I got my raincoat from the closet and_____it_____ before I left the apartment because it looked like rain.

14. I received some important news yesterday which I didn't want to forget, so I_____it_____in my notebook.

15. I didn't remember the definition of the word, so I_____it_____.

16. I'll do my work later. For now, I'm going to_____it_____.

17. I accidentally dropped my pen. Could you please_____it_____for me?

18. Imagine my surprise when I_____ my old friend at the picnic.

19. Since I don't need this piece of paper anymore. I'm going to _____ it _____ now.

20. Last week I told a story that wasn't true about Charles. I _____ it _____.

21. I can't hear the CD properly. Could you please _____ it _____ a little?

22. Before I bought these gorgeous, fashionable shoes, I _____ them _____.

23. If you're looking for your coat, it's in the closet. I _____ it _____.

24. When I was finished working with the tools, I _____ them _____.

25. Since there was no name on the paper, I _____ it _____ and _____ the back to try to identify it.

26. Before you submit the university application, _____ it carefully to make sure you've _____ it _____ completely and accurately.

27. How much does it cost you to _____ your gas tank each week?

28. I made a mistake on the note I wrote you, so I _____ it _____ and wrote you another one.

29. An old building obstructed the construction of the new highway through the city, so they _____ the old building _____ last month.

30. Jim needed the latest sales figures for a presentation, so I went to my computer and quickly _____ a new expenses list.

31. We're lost because I think we've been going in the wrong direction for an hour. Let's _____.

32. I made a mistake in my last essay, so I _____ it _____.

33. If you read your essay over carefully to identify mistakes, you _____ it.

34. Once you finish writing something on the computer, you _____ it _____ to create a hard copy.

Check your answers with the answer key on page 155

List four decisions you made recently or in the past.
Choose one.
Write about it.

Use the phrasal verbs from the structure chart on pp. 62 - 63.
For a comprehensive list of common phrasal verbs, refer to the reference chart on pp. 67 - 69

For editing services, email your writing as a WORD document to:
editessentials@aol.com

Phrasal Verbs

blow up	explode
blow up	get angry
blow down	destroy by wind
blow over	be forgotten
blow out	extinguish
break in	force open
break out	erupt
break up	end a relationship
break down	stop functioning
bring on	cause
bring about	cause
bring up	begin to talk about
bring up	raise children
bring down	cause to fail
care for	take charge of
care for	love
care about	have interest in
carry on	continue
carry on	misbehave
carry out	follow plans
carry through	finish
catch on	understand
catch up	reach the others
close up	end the business day
close down	end the business
close in	surround
close out	stop selling an item
come out	join society
come down on	punish
come through	be reliable
come about	happen
come over	affect
do in	beat up
do up	improve
do over	remodel
drop in	visit without notice
drop by	visit without notice
drop out	stop going to school
fall out	shed
fall out	have a disagreement
fall off	fall from a height
fall down	fall to the ground
fall through	not happen as planned
fall for	accept naively
fall in	associate with a group
fall over	faint
get over	recover
get around	avoid
get through	finish
get by	survive
get on	start
get with	be aware
get about	move
get in	enter
get out	be dismissed, derive
get out	remove
give in	surrender to pressure
give up	stop making an effort
give out	distribute
go on	happen
go for	like a lot
go with	look good with
go with	date steadily
go out	socialize
go in for	take interest in
go out for	compete for a team
go through	suffer
go through	sort
go by	pass
go about	how to handle
go around	not direct
hand in	give to an authority
hand out	distribute
hand over	give under duress

Phrasal Verbs

hang out	*relax*	pass on	*tell others*
hang around	*linger idly*	pass by	*ignore*
hang up	*put clothing on hanger*	pass for	*be accepted falsely*
hang up	*end a phone call*	pass in	*give to an authority*
		pass over	*not promote*
have on	*be wearing*	pass through	*visit on the way*
have to	*must*	pass out	*lose consciousness*
have over	*invite to one's home*	pass up	*miss an opportunity*
hear of	*know about*	pick up	*put in your hands*
hear from	*get news of*	pick up	*collect*
		pick up	*give a ride to*
keep on	*continue*	pick out	*select*
keep away	*not get close*	pick over	*choose carefully*
keep off	*not tread on*	pick on	*selectively mistreat*
keep out	*not enter*	pick at	*scratch*
keep in	*not allow out*		
keep up	*stay apace*	put on	*begin to wear*
keep at	*not stop*	put off	*postpone*
keep for	*reserve*	put out	*extinguish*
		put down	*release, insult*
kick around	*abuse*	put through	*allow contact*
kick out	*dismiss*		
kick in	*add help*	run around	*unfocused socializing*
kick over	*think about*	run into	*meet by accident*
		run for	*seek election*
live for	*love*	run out of	*exhaust a supply of*
live to	*enjoy*	run up	*spend a lot*
live on	*continue living*	run by	*tell something*
live on	*depend on for life*	run over	*go over with a vehicle*
live through	*suffer*	run down	*not take care of*
look for	*search*	see to	*take responsibility*
look at	*observe*	see through	*detect truth*
look through	*examine and search*	see through	*not abandon*
look over	*scan*		
look into	*investigate*	show up	*appear*
look around	*observe*	show through	*be visible*
look over	*observe for selection*	show around	*take on a tour*
look in	*check*		
look out	*be careful*	stand up	*be erect on your feet*
look up	*search for information*	stand for	*mean*
look after	*take care of*	stand for	*believe in*
look down on	*feel superior to*	stand for	*allow*
look up to	*respect*	stand out	*look different*

Phrasal Verbs

stand in	*substitute*	throw out	*discard*
stand by	*wait*	throw away	*discard*
stand by	*give support*	throw over	*remove from power*
		throw up	*vomit*
take in	*make smaller*		
take in	*give shelter to*	tie in	*relate*
take off	*remove*	tie on	*attach with a cord*
take off	*leave*	tie up	*immobilize*
take off	*not go to work*	tie up	*put a cord around*
take for	*believe to be*		
take on	*accept responsibility*	try to	*make an effort*
take up	*pursue an interest*	try on	*put on to test*
take up	*make shorter*	try out	*use to test*
take down	*write an account of*	try out	*audition*
take out	*invite to go out*		
take over	*assume responsibility*	turn on	*start a machine/light*
take around	*give a tour*	turn out	*end a machine/light*
		turn out	*extinguish a light*
tear up	*destroy*	turn off	*extinguish a light*
tear down	*destroy*		
tear out	*remove*	turn to	*ask for help from*
		turn out	*end*
think of	*have in mind*	turn up	*appear unexpectedly*
think about	*have in mind*	turn in	*go to bed*
think through	*consider carefully*	turn down	*refuse an offer*
think over	*consider carefully*	turn over	*move halfway around*
think up	*invent*	turn away	*face a different direction*
		wear off	*waning effect*
		wear out	*become useless*

More Complex Sentence Samples Using Phrasal Verbs

Because we had a great success in our business this week,
we are going to *have* the entire company *over* to our house this weekend to celebrate.

Keep up the good work, John. You will be promoted
if you *see to* your tasks diligently from now to the end of the project.

When the report is finally completed, we will need to *run* it *by*
the company chairman, for him to *look* it *over* thoroughly.

Don't *pass up* the opportunity to *take over* the business
as you *think through* the idea of expanding it.

Phrasal Verbs

Some phrasal verbs have multiple meanings depending on how the phrase is used.

put on
    placing something on the body
    I put on my coat before I went outside.
    applying something to another surface
    He put the book on the table.
    affixing something to another thing
    She hung the picture on the wall.
    gaining weight
    After he ate the meal, he put on some pounds.
    performing a play or other entertainment
    The play was put on in the new theater.
    teasing
    That can't be true! Stop putting me on!

run into
    striking another vehicle
    My car ran into my brother's bicycle.
    meeting someone unexpectedly
    The two friends ran into each other last week.
    experiencing unexpected difficulties
    He ran into trouble while finishing the report.
    when the total grows to a large amount
    The expenses for the house ran into a lot.

take off
    removing something from the body
    She took off her hat when she entered.
    removing something from a surface
    They took the dishes off the table after dinner.
    removing something from something
    it is attached to
    He took the picture off the wall yesterday.
    taking time off from work
    He took time off when he was sick.
    when an airplane leaves the ground
    The plane took off on time.
    when a business becomes successful
    Our business really took off and we made money.
    leaving suddenly
    It got late and we had to take off.
    reducing the price
    The store took 20% off the price.

come off (it)
    becoming detached
    The tire came off our car last week.
    creating a success
    Our presentation came off very well.
    rejecting someone's statement
    I can't believe you! Come off it!

go after
    attacking people
    The police went after the criminal.
    a legal procedure
    The lawyer went after the defendant.
    increasing customers
    The business went after new customers.
    trying to achieve a goal
    The team went after the trophy.

break down
    something mechanical does not work
    Our car broke down on the way home.
    the end of an agreement
    Our negotiations broke down yesterday.
    loss of self-control
    She broke down when she heard the news.
    decomposition
    Scientists try to break down materials.
    reducing a process to understand it
    Let's break down the steps we have to follow.
    using force to go through a door
    He broke down the door when he couldn't open it.

look at
    focusing one's eyes on something
    We looked at the falling meteor.
    examing a situation to solve it
    We should look at the details of the problem.
    having a certain opinion
    We should look at all sides of a situation.
    considering an option
    He looked at the possible ways to solve the problem.

Unit 11

Forms

**Structure Chart
Exercises
Writing Practice
References**

Forms

Expressions with DO

do a favor	do your hair
do a job	do the minimum
do a project	do the shopping
do a task	do the ironing
do an assignment	do something
do badly	do the laundry
do business	do the math
do damage	do the maximum
do exercise	do the paperwork
do good	do time
do harm	do your best
do homework	do your duty
do housework	do well
do nothing	do the cleaning
do research	do something
do work	do the accounts
do the dishes	do the vacuuming

Expressions with MAKE

make the bed	make a list
make a cake	make a living
make a change	make a mess
make a choice	make a mistake
make a deal	make money
make a decision	make noise
make a demand	make plans
make an effort	make a point
make an exception	make sure
make excuses	make progress
make friends	make a promise
make an impression	make room
make a speech	make sense
make a suggestion	make trouble
make fun	make peace
make merry	make a fuss
make a meal	make arrangements

Expressions with HAVE

have a drink	have breakfast
have a party	have a talk
have a nice time	have a fight
have fun	have a look
have a ball	have a peek

Expressions with TAKE

take a shower	take a guess
take a vacation	take a deep breath
take a rest	take a break
take a walk	take a nap
take a look	take advantage
take a chance	take care
take back responsibility	take a risk
take place	take your time
take exams	take part
take a taxi	take for granted
take offense	take it easy
take on	take cover
take over	take a job
take a swim	take a hike
	take a trip

Expressions with GET

get a good mark	get upset
get a shock	get to a place
get an idea	get in trouble
get angry	get in touch
get lost	get a haircut
get off	get ready
get on	get married
get on well	get to the bottom
get rid of something	get along
get away	get it
get back	get out of
get going	get over
get into	get up
get through	get in
get by	get down
get up	get around
get excited	get cold
get promoted	get tired
get bored	get hired
get sick	get used to
get well	get rewarded
get a ride	get past

*Complete the sentences with the correct forms of **make** or **do**. Use appropriate tenses.*

1. I'll be back a little later after I_____the grocery shopping.
2. In order to really succeed, you will have to_____more of an effort.
3. Even though I didn't win the prize, I was proud I_____my best.
4. I spent the last two hours _____enquiries about tours of San Diego.
5. Although you want to help us, you are_____more harm than good.
6. Even though we should tell them about it, it's not worth_____a big fuss.
7. Have you_____all the necessary arrangements for the journey?
8. I don't enjoy going to parties but for you I will_____an exception.
9. The visitors_____a terrible mess while we were gone.
10. The football fans _____a lot of damage after the match last week.
11. It is important to_____the right decision in choosing a career.
12. Would you _____me a favor and fill out this form completely?
13. Everyone who came to the park yesterday_____a big effort to help.
14. What do you_____for a living?
15. He had not_____his homework before he went to the football practice.
16. I can't give you the answer at the moment. I'll have to_____some research.
17. We'll have to work diligently if we want to _____significant progress.
18. It's not easy to_____business with people from different cultures.

*Complete the sentences with the correct forms of **take** and appropriate prepositions.*

19. This idea became a huge success. The way it_____was gratifying.
20. I'm so busy right now that I can't conceive of_____any new projects.
21. Since it's broken, I have to_____it_____to the store for a refund.

22. I'm really sorry about what I said last week. I wish I could_____it_____.

23. He has really worked hard recently so he deserves to_____.

24. When a person is tired, he needs to_____to restore his energy level.

Complete the sentences with the correct forms of *get*. Use appropriate tenses, word forms and prepositions where needed.

25. When he lost his job, he had a hard time_____it.

26. Hurry and eat or your dinner before it_____.

27. Did you hear about the idea of _____cheaper phone calls soon?

28. She always_____the bus to work during the winter months.

29. We're going to the beach, so I'll_____you around 8:00 a.m.

30. I don't_____with my professor, even though I try.

31. What really_____me is how he insists he is always right.

32. He_____very easily, so be careful not to make him mad.

33. Our order is ready to be picked up. I'll_____it.

34. I think he is a very strange person and I never really_____him.

35. It's good that John _____ a job at last. He's been unemployed for a while.

36. I've been trying to talk to Joan all day, but I can't_____her by phone.

37. Did you_____the Tower of London on your trip to England?

38. How long did it take you to_____to Thailand last winter?

39. Have you ever_____a sting from a jelly fish?

40. It is not necessary to_____angry over small things.

41. If you_____up early, you'll _____to work on time.

Check your answers with the answer key on page 155

Select one of the following scenarios and write about it.
Combine a real person or character with characters he or she is unlikely to meet.
Imagine one or more real people or characters in an unlikely setting.
Imagine a real person or character having a minor mishap.

Use the forms on the structure chart on p. 72 to create your scenario.
Refer to the reference chart on p. 76 to study other forms
often used in English to add interest to your writing.

For editing services, email your writing as a WORD document to:
editessentials@aol.com

Forms

Take & Bring

To *take* means to carry something away to another person or area.
Take these books to Room 14.

To *bring* means to have someone carry something to the place where you are.
Bring me the exam sheets.

Say & Tell

To *say* something means to make a general statement.
Paul *said* that he was working hard.

To *tell* means to make a specific statement with information.
The director *told* us the company was being sold.

Borrow & Lend

To *borrow* means to temporarily take something from a person or place.
She *borrowed* my pen to complete her work.

To *lend* means to give something to someone temporarily.
I *lent* her my pen to complete her work.

Until & Up To

Until indicates a period of time before something happens.
I will wait until this afternoon.
Up to indicates either a period of time or a distance.
I will wait up to 5:00 o'clock.
I will walk up to the road with you.

As Far As & As Long As

As far as indicates a distance.
I will go with you as far as the bridge.
As long as indicates time.
I will help you as long as you need me to.

Used to/Get Used to/Be used to

Used to describes something done in the past. *I used to ride my bicycle.*
Get used to describes a process of becoming accustomed to something. *I got used to walking.*
Be used to describes a completed process of having become accustomed to something.
I'm used to getting up early.

Hope & Wish

To *hope* means to believe that it is possible for something you want to come true because you have done something to prepare for it.
I *hope* to pass my algebra course. I've been working very hard.

To *wish* means to want something for which you have not done anything to make the result possible.
I *wish* I could go to Italy this summer, but I haven't saved enough money.

Glance, See, Look, Watch, Stare, Peer & Gaze

To *glance* means to look at something very quickly without really noticing it.
To *see* means to notice without paying specific attention.
To *look* means to deliberately focus on something specific.
To *watch* means to look at something specific for a period of time.
To *stare* means to look at with concentration.
To *peer* means to look intensely at a specific thing to discover something about it.
To *gaze* means to look at without overt consciousness.

Unit 12

Clauses

Structure Chart
Exercises
Writing Practice
References

Time Relationships

after	*After* she graduates, she will get a job.
before	I will leave *before* he comes.
when	*When* it began to rain, I stood under a tree.
while as	*While/as* I was walking home, it began to rain.
by the time	*By the time* he arrives, we will already have left.
since	I haven't seen him *since* he left this morning.
until till	We stayed there *until/till* we finished our work.
as soon as once	*As soon as/once* it stops raining, we will leave.
as long as so long as	I will never do that again *as long as/so long as* I live.
whenever every time	*Whenever/every time* I meet him, I say hello.
the first time	*The first time* I went to NY, I went to an opera.
the last time	I saw two plays *the last time* I went to New York.
the next time	*The next time* I go to NY, I will go to a ballet.

Cause & Effect

because	He went to bed *because* he was sleepy.
now that	*Now that* the course is over, I'm going to rest.
since	*Since* Monday is a holiday, I'm going to go shopping.

Contrast

while	Mary is rich, *while* John is poor.
although even though though	*Although, even though, though* the weather was cold, I went swimming.

Condition

whether or not	I'm going swimming today *whether or not* it is cold.
even if	I'm going swimming today *even if* it is cold.
in case in the event that	I'll be at home tonight *in case / in the event that* you want to visit.
only if	The picnic will be cancelled *only if* it rains.
unless	I'll go swimming tomorrow *unless* it rains.
in spite of the fact that	*In spite of the fact that* he is not finished, he will come.
in spite of despite	*In spite of/despite* the weather, we went walking.
despite the fact that regardless of the fact that	*Despite the fact that/regardless of the fact that* he was tired, he ran the race.

Combine each pair of sentences with the words in parentheses.

1. The commissioner will arrive at noon. We'll start the meeting. *(as soon as)*

2. I read the book quickly. I borrowed the book from the library. *(after)*

3. He gives many excellent presentations. He visits different companies. *(whenever)*

4. We were leaving for Honolulu. We got the news about the free trip. *(just as)*

5. They had to stay at the airport overnight. The weather cleared up. *(until)*

6. I went jet-skiing in Hawaii. I felt exhilarated. *(the first time)*

7. We can continue studying for our degree. We have completed the required courses. *(now that)*

8. We decided to postpone the beach party. The weather had been inclement all week. *(since)*

9. The language course was very difficult for him. He had not done the preliminary work. *(because)*

Complete the sentences with your own words.

10. Now that I'm finally ready to_____.

11. Since it's too late to_____.

12. Gary needs to be home early now that_____.

Choose the correct completion.

13. Because it was a brilliant, clear afternoon,_____

    (a) I didn't need to put on my sunglasses
    (b) I needed to put on my sunglasses

14. Even though it was a brilliant, clear afternoon,_____

    (a) I needed to put on my sunglasses
    (b) I didn't need to put on my sunglasses

Choose the sentence that has the same meaning as the given sentence.

16. Even if I get an engraved invitation to the company reception, I'm not going to attend.

    (a) I won't go to the reception unless I get a personal invitation.

    (b) It doesn't matter whether or not I get an invitation, I'm not planning to go.

17. I need to work on my project tomorrow whether I feel better or not.

    (a) Whether I work on my project or not depends on how I feel.

    (b) I'm going to work on my project tomorrow no matter how I feel.

*Make sentences with the same meaning as the given sentences. Use **unless**.*

18. You can't visit other countries and return to your own country officially if you don't have a passport.

    _____

19. You can't pass the driver's test if you're not at least sixteen years old and can follow the rules of the road.

    _____

20. Noone can remain in good health if they don't eat healthy food and do exercises.

    _____

Read the situations and complete the sentences.

Situation: *If you want to go walking in the park, we'll go. If you don't want to go, we won't go.*

_____

Situation: *You have to buy a season ticket. Then you can always get into the soccer stadium for any match.*

_____

Situation: *I have to get a good job. Then I will have enough money to buy a new car.*

_____

Check your answers with the answer key on page 155

What do you dream of doing?
Write down five of your dreams.
Choose one.
Write about it.

*Use the clauses listed on the structure chart on p. 80 to write your paragraph.
Examine the additional noun clauses and adjective clauses on the reference chart on p. 82.*

*For editing services, email your writing as a WORD document to:
editessentials@aol.com*

Noun Clauses

A noun clause has the same uses in a sentence as a noun.
It is used as an object or a subject.

Basic Noun Clauses

I know *what he said*. Object of know.

What he said is true. Subject of is.

Noun Clauses Beginning with Question Words

I don't know *where she lives*.
I don't know *why she came*.
I didn't hear *what he said*.
We don't know *how he did his work*.
Do you know *when they arrive*?
I don't know *who lives there*.

Noun Clauses with Whether & If

I don't know *whether she will come*.
I wonder *if he needs help*.
Whether she comes or not is unimportant.

Noun Clauses with That Following Verbs

agree that	feel that
believe that	find out that
decide that	forget that
discover that	hear that
explain that	hope that

Noun Clauses with That Following Adjectives

afraid that	amazed that
angry that	aware that
certain that	confident that
disappointed that	glad that

Adjective Clauses

As Subject

The book *which* is on the table is mine.

The book *that* is on the table is mine.

The man *who* came early is my friend.

As Object of Verb

The movie *which* we saw last night was interesting.
The movie *that* we saw last night was interesting.
The man *whom* we met is my friend.

Where & When in Adjective Clauses

The building *where* he lives is very old.

The building *in which* he lives is very old.

I'll never forget the day *when* I met you.

I'll never forget the day *on which* we met.

As Object of Preposition

She is the woman *about whom* I told you.

She is the woman *whom* I told you *about*.

The music *to which* we listened was good.

The music *that* we listened *to* was good.

Unit 13

Sentence Combining

Sentence Combining

Sentence combining is the organization of short sentences into longer, more effective sentences, in order to develop versatility in written expression.

She was our favorite teacher.
We were in elementary school.
She was tall and thin.
Her complexion was fair.
She had dark eyes.
Her eyes were sparkling.
Her hair was blond.

Our favorite elementary school teacher was a tall, thin woman with sparkling dark eyes, a fair complexion, and blond hair.

Adding Adjectives & Adverbs to the Basic Sentence Unit

A man gave me a drawing.
It was of a young woman.
He did this silently.
He did it tenderly.
The man was old.
The drawing was beautiful.
It had torn edges.
It was faded.
The woman's eyes were sad.
The drawing brought back memories.
It brought back instant memories.
They were lovely memories.
They were from a long time ago.
The memories made me happy.

An old man silently and tenderly gave me a beautiful, faded drawing with torn edges, of a young woman with sad eyes, that instantly brought back lovely memories from a long time ago, making me happy.

Adding Prepositional Phrases to the Basic Sentence Unit

We traveled this past summer.
We traveled by train.
We also traveled by car.
We traveled from our home.
We traveled to my father's home.
It was a good trip.
We were glad to see our father.

This past summer we had a good trip traveling by car and by train from our home to my father's home to see him again.

Anthony played.
Anthony played at home.
He played behind the sofa.
He was with his friend.
His friend was imaginary.
They played for hours.
Nobody watched them.
Nobody knew they were there.

Anthony played for hours at home behind the sofa with his imaginary friend while nobody watched them and nobody knew they were there.

A man stood, looking down.
He stood on a railroad bridge.
The bridge was in Kentucky.
He was looking down into the water.
The water was twenty feet below.
The water was swift.
The water was turbulent.

A man stood on a railroad bridge in Kentucky, looking down into the swift turbulent water twenty feet below.

Sentence Combining

I climbed onto the swing.
I did this one night.
The night was hot.
The night was in summer.
The night was in 1979.
It was my favorite swing.
My swing was in the park.
The park was lovely.
The swing was on a hill.
The swing was wooden.
The park was in South Salem.
Nobody else was playing there.
I was all alone.
It was raining.

On a hot and rainy summer night in 1979, I climbed onto my favorite wooden swing set on a hill in a lovely park in South Salem, all alone because noone else was there that night.

Adding Coordinating Words, Phrases & Clauses to the Basic Sentence Unit

The winds dispersed.
The winds became gentle.
The rain slackened to a drizzle
The rain became a mist.
The clouds parted.
The clouds cleared.
The sun shone through.
It was a beautiful day.
I was outside.
I was in our garden.

I was outside in our garden when the winds dispersed and became gentle, the rain slackened to a drizzle and a mist, and the clouds parted, then cleared, letting the sun shine through, making it a beautiful day.

The sun dries the dew.
The dew is on the grass.
The grass is in the park.
The sun warms us.
The sun bakes us.
The sun makes us brown.
The sun makes us hot.
The sun makes us thirsty.
We go inside.
It is cool inside.
There is water inside.
It refreshes us.

The sun dries the dew on the grass in the park and warms us, baking us and making us brown and hot, making us thirsty until we go into the cool interior to find water to refresh ourselves.

Adding Adverb Clauses to the Basic Sentence Unit

Some day I shall wander.
I shall never return.
I shall go out into the meadow.
The meadow is behind the house.
The meadow is beautiful.
I shall do this deliberately.
I shall do this when the clouds are low.
I shall do this when the clouds are ominous.
I shall do this when the rain is streaming down.
I shall do this when the wind is wild.

Some day, when the clouds are low and ominous, the rain is streaming down, and the wind is wild, I shall go out deliberately into the beautiful meadow behind the house, to wander, never to return.

Combine the shorter sentences into one or two longer sentences.

1. I lived alone.
   I lived in the woods.
   I lived a mile from any neighbor.
   I lived in a house I built myself.
   I lived there for two years.

2. Human nature has a fine quality.
   It is similar to ripe fruit.
   It must be handled delicately.
   We do not treat ourselves tenderly.
   We do not treat one another kindly.

3. Most people live in desperation.
   This desperation is quiet.
   It is resignation.
   It is an unconscious despair.
   It is hidden by the pursuit of idle entertainment.

4. We must consider what the chief purpose of mankind is.
It is not too late.
We have to give up prejudices.
We have to have proof.
None of our thinking can be trusted.
What is true today, may not be true tomorrow.

5. I have been anxious to value time.
I have appreciated it in any weather.
I have appreciated it at any time.
I have stood on the edge of eternity.
The past and the future have met.
That is the present moment.

6. We want to succeed.
We are in a hurry to become successful.
We do not need to keep up with anyone.
We need to consider our own thoughts.
We need to follow our own paths.

Check your answers with the possibilities on page 90

What thoughts do you have about life?
Determine if your view of life is optimistic or pessimistic.
Describe your view about life.
Write about it thoughtfully.

*Use sentence combinations similar to the ones shown on the structure chart on p. 84 - 85
to write your description.
Examine the additional features of combined sentences on the reference chart on p. 89 - 90.*

*For editing services, email your writing as a WORD document to:
editessentials@aol.com*

Evaluating Sentence Combining

Meaning (1)	Clarity (4)
It is important to express the idea intended by the original author.	The sentence must be understood when first read.
Coherence (2)	**Emphasis (5)**
The parts of the sentence must fit together logically and smoothly.	The key words and phrases must be in order of importance.
Conciseness (3)	**Rhythm (6)**
The sentence must express an idea without wasting words.	The sentence must have flow and must move smoothly.

Evaluate the following combined sentences for the features listed above.

Sentence	1	2	3	4	5	6
A man stood on a railroad bridge in Kentucky, looking down into the swift turbulent water twenty feet below.						
On a hot and rainy summer night last year, he walked blissfully along the river bank, all alone, because noone else was there that night.						
She was on a garden walk when the wind whipped up, the rain streamed down, fiercely hitting her face, and chilling her to the bone.						
The rising sun illuminated the pond in its stillness, and shone its light onto every tree in the forest.						
What we think today is not necessarily what we believe another day, when we have gained more experience.						

Sample Answers for Sentence Combining Exercises

1. I lived in the woods alone for two years, a mile from any neighbor, in a house I built myself.

   For two years, I lived in the woods alone, in a house I built myself, a mile from any neighbor.

   For two years, I lived alone in the woods, a mile from any neighbor, in a house I built myself.

2. The quality of human nature is similar to ripe fruit, and must be handled delicately, as we treat ourselves tenderly and one another kindly.

   Human nature has the quality of ripe fruit, needing to be handled delicately, as we treat ourselves and one another tenderly and kindly.

   Human nature has a fine quality similar to ripe fruit and needs to be handled delicately in our treatment of ourselves and others with kindness and tenderness.

3. Most people live in quiet desperation, in a kind of resignation, an unconscious despair, which they try to hide by pursuing idle entertainment.

   Most people experience a kind of resignation, a quiet desperation and an unconscious despair, which they ignore by engaging in constant entertainment.

4. It is not too late to consider what the chief purpose of mankind is, as we give up our prejudices, not trusting our own thinking, which may be true today but may not be true tomorrow.

   It is not too late to consider what the chief purpose of mankind is, relinquishing our prejudices, and not trusting our thinking, because it may not be true tomorrow even if it is true today.

5. I have been anxious to value time in any weather, at any time, having stood on the edge of eternity, where the past and the future meet in the present moment.

   To value time at any time, in any kind of weather, is to stand on the edge of eternity, allowing the present moment to intertwine the past with the future.

6. In our desire to become successful, we attempt to keep up with others, but we need only to consider our own thoughts, and to follow our own paths.

   We need not keep with others to succeed, but only to follow our own thoughts and paths.

Unit 14

Parallel Structure

Variations of Parallel Structure

Parallel structure is used with a series of items to produce concise and balanced meaning. Parallelism creates economy and clarity of language, equality in terms of importance of ideas, and rhythm in expression, to create a sense of pleasure through control of the language.

Parallelism with Nouns

Faulty: The wind blew, the rain fell, and it was bad weather.
Correct: The wind blew, the rain fell, and the weather was bad.

Parallelism with Prepositional Phrases

Faulty: The sun shone on the garden, the trees and in the water.
Correct: The sun shone on the garden, on the trees and on the water.

Parallelism with Adjectives

Faulty: The vacation was pleasant, entertaining, and we did a lot of things.
Correct: The vacation was pleasant, entertaining and active.

Parallelism with Independent Clauses

Faulty: The people voted to build a new library, but don't know how to finance it.
Correct: The people voted to build a new library, but they didn't know how to finance it.

Parallelism with Adverbs

Faulty: They worked hard, carefully and with energy.
Correct: They worked hard, carefully and energetically.

Parallelism with Subordinate Clauses

Faulty: She graduated from school with honors, before she had gone to live in Europe.
Correct: She graduated from school with honors, before she went to live in Europe.

Parallelism with Verb Tenses

Faulty: We walked through the woods, picked wild blueberries, and are now home.
Correct: We walked through the woods, picked wild blueberries, and went home.

Parallelism with Coordinating Conjunctions

Faulty: The winter arrived suddenly and with bitter cold.
Correct: The winter arrived suddenly and brought bitter cold with it.

Parallelism with Gerunds

Faulty: Reading, listening to music and to watch TV are relaxing.
Correct: Reading, listening to music and watching TV are relaxing.

Parallelism with Correlative Conjunctions

Faulty: He not only studied ancient languages, but also ancient history.
Correct: He studied not only ancient languages, but also ancient history.

Parallelism with Infinitives

Faulty: I want to travel, visit historical sites, and learn about different cultures.
Correct: I want to travel, to visit historical sites, and to learn about different cultures.

Parallelism with a Series

Faulty: It was a great day, a wonderful night, and we enjoyed it.
Correct: It was a great day, a wonderful night, and an enjoyable time.

Parallelism with Comparisons

Faulty: He would rather sail the ocean than going whitewater rafting.
Correct: He would rather sail the ocean than go whitewater rafting.

Parallelism with Linking Verbs

Faulty: He appeared to be a success, and was proud.
Correct: He appeared to be a success, and to be a proud man.

Identify the sentences with the correct parallel structure.

1. ○ (a) The meeting will begin at noon and we will start the negotiations then.
   ○ (b) The meeting will begin at noon and the negotiations soon after that.

2. ○ (a) I read the book quickly after I borrowed it from my friend.
   ○ (b) I read the book quickly after my friend lent it to me.

3. ○ (a) He gives many excellent presentations when he visits different companies.
   ○ (b) He gives many excellent presentations on visiting different companies.

4. ○ (a) We were leaving for Honolulu, got the news about the free trip, arranged our flight, and we had a good time.
   ○ (b) We were leaving for Honolulu, got the news about the free trip, arranged our flight, and were sure we would have a good time.

5. ○ (a) They had to stay at the airport overnight until the weather cleared up.
   ○ (b) They had to stay at the airport overnight and the weather cleared up.

6. ○ (a) The first time I went jet-skiing in Hawaii, I felt exhilarated and full of pride.
   ○ (b) The first time I went jet-skiing in Hawaii, I felt exhilarated and proud.

7. ○ (a) We can continue studying for our degree or we have completed the required courses.
   ○ (b) We can continue studying for our degree or complete the required courses.

8. ○ (a) We decided to postpone the party on the beach because the rain had been falling on the village all week.
   ○ (b) We decided to postpone the party on the beach because of the rain on the village.

Edit the faulty parallelism in the following sentences.

9. The speaker had chosen to give a fine speech, but the audience doesn't want to listen to him.

   _____

10. Because it was a brilliant, clear afternoon, we decided to go to the fair to ride the ferris wheel, buy ice cream and spending the day having fun.

    _____

11. In the afternoon, and evening, we walked along the shore, watched the waves.

    _____

12. Even if I get an engraved invitation to the company reception, with a gold ring, I'm not going to attend because of not enjoying parties.

   _____

   _____

13. I need to work on my project tomorrow whether I feel better or worse.

   _____

Choose one of the sentence completions to create a parallel sentence.

14. You can't visit other countries_____ if you don't have a passport.

    (a) nor return to your own country
    (b) or get back home
    (c) or have a good time

15. You can't pass the driver's test if you're not at least sixteen years old and_____.

    (a) if you can't pass the rules of the road
    (b) unless you pass the rules of the road
    (c) able to pass the rules of the road

16. Noone can remain in good health _____ and do exercises.

    (a) if they don't eat healthy food
    (b) unless they eat healthy food
    (c) who doesn't eat healthy food

17. The young couple were married on a bright, sunny day, traveled to Costa Rica that night, and _____ their new life.

    (a) happily celebrated
    (b) were happily celebrating
    (c) could happily celebrate

18. Once upon a time, in a land far away, _____there lived a wizard with remarkable powers that transformed the landscape into a magical land.

    (a) in the distant past
    (b) long ago
    (c) time out of mind

Check your answers with the answer key on page 155

Write various sentences describing different aspects of your life and thoughts.
Describe your inner feelings about several topics.
Create sentences which touch the reader in some way
and make him feel what you are describing.

Use different parallel structures similar to the ones shown on the chart on p. 92
to write your descriptions.
Examine the additional samples of parallelism on the reference chart on p. 96

For editing services, email your writing as a WORD document to:
editessentials@aol.com

Sample Parallel Structure Sentences

I have occasional visits in the long winter evenings, when the snow falls fast and the wind howls in the woods.

At length the winter came in good earnest, and the wind began to howl around the house, as if it had not had permission to do so before.

Sometimes I rambled further westward, or, while the sun was setting, made a supper of blueberries on the hill.

On warm evenings, I frequently sat in my boat playing the flute, and saw the moon traveling over the water.

The pond was completely surrounded by thick and lofty pines and oaks, and in some of its coves grape vines had run over the trees next to the water and formed bowers under which a boat could pass.

The rain was now over, and a rainbow above the eastern woods promised a fair evening, so I set out on my journey gladly and with anticipation.

My house was on the side of a hill, on the edge of the large wood, in the middle of a young forest of pines, near the pond, to which a narrow path led down the hill.

I have a tight house, ten feet wide by fifteen long, and eight feet posts, with a garret and a closet, a large window on each side, two trap doors, one door at the end and a brick fireplace.

This small lake was of most value during a gentle rainstorm in August, both air and water being perfectly still, the sky overcast and the evening serene.

A lake like this is never smoother than at such a time, made shallow and dark by clouds, with the water full of light and reflection.

The light which puts out our eyes is darkness to us and only that day dawns to which we are awake, since there is more day to dawn, the sun being but a morning star.

The life in us is like the water in the river, rising higher this year than man has ever known, and flooding the parched uplands.

Rather than love, than money, than fame, give me truth.

From *Walden*
Henry David Thoreau

Unit 15

Sentence Variety

Techniques for Creating Variety in Sentences

Sentence variety can be created by using the four basic sentence types alternately throughout the writing.
Another way of creating variety is to use different techniques to create new forms.

Variety in Length of Sentences

She called out suddenly. In his surprise, he did not immediately realize that she needed his help.

Variety in Sentence Beginnings

Adverb	Suddenly the rain began to pour down.
Prepositional Phrase	In the evening, they played cards.
Adjective	Beautiful and calm, the lake shimmered.
Present Participial Phrase	Deciding to go for a walk, they set out early.
Past Participial Phrase	Delapidated and torn, the gate swung loosely.
Adverb Clause	Despite the lateness of the hour, they still read.
Verb	Try hard to succeed.
Gerund	Loving our children is a great joy.
Infinitive	To begin a new day is a pleasure.
Correlative Conjunction	Whether or not we go to town is not important.
Subject	The dawn surprised us with its brilliant colors.

Variety in Repetition

The quiet end of the day, when the sunset colored the whole world, the sunset that we had awaited eagerly all day, the sunset that we had thought we would never see again, gave us a strange peace.

Variety in Transitions

Using different transitional vocabulary with similar meanings creates variety in sentences.
however, moreover, nevertheless, but, therefore

Placing various transitions in different positions in the sentence produces variety.

Variety through -ing/ed Joining

He thought the day would never end, feeling as though he had traveled a great distance, and noticing that the end of the journey was approaching.

He thought the day would never end, troubled and disturbed in his impression that the road, long traveled, would continue forever.

Variety through Modifiers

Appositives

The man, the one who had given her the roses, met her at the gate.

Relative Clause

The woman who had given me her umbrella joined us on our walk.

Beginning with a Modifier

Violent but beautiful, the storm came suddenly, surprising us.

Ending with a Modifier

The road appeared long and desolate before us, wandering continuously uphill.

Placing a Modifier in the Middle

The forest, dark, dim and dense, presented a frightening appearance.

Modifier chain

The boy, small and helpless, not much older than ten, but wiry and athletic, jumped the hurdle easily.

Summative Modifiers

It seemed as if she would stay there forever, watching the ocean waves roll in, sitting quietly on the beach, not knowing that someone was watching her from the path.

Select the sentence with the best sense of variety and clarity.

1. ○ (a) The young man, whose manner was extremely elegant, rose to greet us.
   ○ (b) The young man with the extremely elegant manner rose to greet us.

2. ○ (a) A dark cloud blocked the sun, so John put away his camera.
   ○ (b) John put away his camera when a dark cloud blocked the sun.

3. ○ (a) We went on a vacation, which began last week, and had a lot of fun.
   ○ (b) Our vacation, which began last week, was a lot of fun.

4. ○ (a) Because we weren't aware of the approaching storm, we drove to the beach and had a picnic anyway.
   ○ (b) Even though we weren't aware of the approaching storm, we drove to the beach and had a picnic.

5. ○ (a) Some of us found the lecturer boring, so we left the auditorium.
   ○ (b) Those of us who found the lecturer boring, left the auditorium.

6. ○ (a) We had a great party: full of fun, good food and companionship.
   ○ (b) We had a great party that was full of fun, good food and companionship.

Choose the sentence which best revises the model sentence for clarity and conciseness.

7. *Susan was discouraged about her studies. She was not able to continue her courses. She decided to quit.*

   ○ (a) Susan was not able to continue her courses, and decided to quit because she was discouraged about her studies.
   ○ (b) Because she was discouraged about her studies, Susan quit her studies and was not able to continue her courses

8. *While walking in the mountains, John stepped into a gopher hole. He twisted his ankle. That made it difficult for him to continue his hike.*

   ○ (a) While he was walking in the mountains, John found it difficult to continue his hike after he stepped into a gopher hole and twisted his ankle.
   ○ (b) While walking the mountains, John stepped into a gopher hole and twisted his ankle, making it difficult for him to continue his hike.

9. *In the afternoon, and in the early evening, we walked along the shore and watched the waves roll in.*

   ○ (a) We walked along the shore in the afternoon and early evening, watching the waves roll in.
   ○ (b) Watching the waves roll in, we walked along the shore in the afternoon and early evening.

Select the best beginning for each sentence.

10. _____the bad weather, we decided to leave on our journey.

    (a)   In spite of
    (b)   Although

11. _____the storm tore down the old tree which had been there for a hundred years.

    (a)   In the dead of night
    (b)   At the edge of the garden

12. _____the diamond necklace was her most precious possession.

    (a)   No matter what
    (b)   Bright and gleaming

Choose the best modifier for each sentence.

13. _____he wrapped his coat about himself and set off for the town.

    (a)   desolate and cold
    (b)   quiet and lonely

14. He was startled by the _____ of thunder and the _____of the lightning that came up from the south.

    (a)   distant sound...bright glow
    (b)   sudden rumble...vicious stab

15. She had never before seen such a desolate scene,_____.

    (a)   sad and lonely
    (b)   poor and dirty

Expand on the idea in this simple sentence by writing a variety of sentences.

The weather was cold.

_____

_____

_____

Check your answers with the answer key on page 155

Think of various simple ideas expressed in simple sentences.
Expand these ideas into a descriptive paragraph using varied sentences.
Try to develop rhythm and balance in the phrases
so that the writing has interest.

*Use different methods of obtaining sentence variety similar to the ones shown on the chart on p. 98
to write your paragraphs.
Examine the additional samples of sentence variety on the reference chart on p. 102*

*For editing services, email your writing as a WORD document to:
editessentials@aol.com*

Sample Sentences Showing Variety

What a man thinks of himself, that it is which determines, or rather indicates, his fate.

The grand necessity, then, for our bodies, is to keep warm, to keep the vital heat in us.

I am convinced, both by faith and experience, that to maintain one's self on this earth is not a hardship but a pastime, if we will live simply and wisely.

This small lake was of most value as a neighbor in the intervals of a gentle rainstorm in August, when, both air and water being perfectly still, but the sky overcast, mid-afternoon had all the serenity of evening, and the wood thrush sang around, and was heard from shore to shore.

Every morning was a cheerful invitation to make my life of equal simplicity, and I may say innocence, with nature herself.

Morning is when I am awake and there is a dawn in me.

Let us spend one day as deliberately as nature, and not be thrown off the tracks by every nutshell and mosquito's wing that falls on the rails. Let us rise early and fast, gently and without perturbation; let company come and let company go, let the bells ring and the children cry - determined to make a day of it.

Time is but the stream I go fishing in. I drink at it; but while I drink I see the sandy bottom and detect how shallow it is. Its thin current slides away, but eternity remains.

Sometimes on Sundays, I heard the bells, when the wind was favorable, a faint, sweet, and, as it were, natural melody, worth importing into the wilderness.

Some of my pleasantest hours were during the long rainstorms in the spring or fall, which confined me to the house for the afternoon as well as the forenoon, soothed by their ceaseless roar and peltings; when an early twilight ushered in a long evening in which many thoughts had time to take root and unfold themselves.

I find it wholesome to be alone the greater part of the time. To be in company, even with the best, is soon wearisome and dissipating. I love to be alone. I never found the companion that was so companionable as solitude.

From *Walden*
Henry David Thoreau

Unit 16

Idiomatic Expressions

Idiomatic Expressions

A bit much
Something excessive or annoying

A lot on my plate
Very busy

A pretty penny
Very expensive

A steal
Cost much lower than the worth of something

Above board
Something done legally and correctly

Back burner
Something with low priority

Back to square one
Starting a project over

Back to the drawing board
Starting over

Back to the wall
In a difficult situation with few choices

Bad shape
Poor condition

Ball is in your court
It is up to you to make the next decision

Ballpark figure
An estimate of costs

Basket case
Something impossibly bad

Bated breath
Waiting with excitement

Call it a day
Stop working

Call the shots
In charge

Calm before the storm
A calm time before a lot of activity

Can of worms
A lot of trouble

Case by case
Each situation handled separately

Castles in the air
Idealistic plans that will never work out

Dead even
People in a competition with the same score

Dead in the water
Making no progress, hopeless

Dead right
Completely correct

Devil is in the details
Small things and plans often cause a lot of trouble

Eagle eyes
Someone who sees everything

Easy as pie
Very easy

Easy come, easy go
Things that come without effort tend to not work out

Easy does it
Don't approach a task with a lot of intensity and turmoil

Etched in stone
Something very rigid, to be followed precisely

Idiomatic Expressions

Even keel
Balanced approach

Face the music
Accepting negative consequences

Face value
Accepted for its appearance

Fair and square
Following the rules

Game plan
Strategy

Get a handle on
Understanding something

Get cracking
Starting to work

Get if off your chest
Talking about a problem to relieve tension

Get my drift
Understanding what someone is trying to say

Get the ball rolling
Starting a project to make progress

Get the green light
Getting the necessary permission

Get the hang of it
Becoming familiar with something and knowing how to do it

Get the picture
Understanding a situation fully

Get up and go
A lot of enthusiasm and energy

Hang in the balance
Hard to predict which option will win.

Hard act to follow
Difficult to repeat because of value

Hard to come by
Difficult to find

Haste makes waste
If you hurry, you will not succeed

Have a ball
Have a great time

Have a crack
Try something that has proven to be difficult for others

Have a go
Try something from a different perspective

Have a heart
Be kind and sympathetic

Jog my memory
Remind me

Jump the gun
To start doing something before the correct time

Jump through hoops
Make great effort and sacrifices

I've got a bone to pick with you
A complaint against the person being addressed

I've got your number
I understand your true nature

Icing on the cake
An additional benefit

Idiomatic Expressions

If worst comes to worst
The worst possible thing could happen

In a fix
In trouble

In a flash
Happening very quickly

In a fog
Confused

In a heartbeat
Happening very quickly

In a nutshell
A succinct summary

In a rut
Doing the same thing repeatedly

In a tight spot
In a difficult situation

In an instant
Very quickly

Keep in touch
Keep communicating

Keep your chin up
Don't get discouraged

Keep your cool
Don't get excited

Keep your fingers crossed
Hope for a positive outcome

Last laugh
Having the advantage in a situation

Last straw
The final problem

Left in the dark
Not informed

Lend an ear
Listen

Lesser of two evils
The less negative choice

Let sleeping dogs lie
Don't ask for trouble

Let the cat out of the bag
Reveal a secret

Let the chips fall where they may
Accept the inevitable

Made in the shade
Things working out easily and well

Make a song and dance
Making an unecessary fuss

Make ends meet
Having trouble living on earnings

Make or break
A decision determining success or failure

Make waves
Cause trouble

Neither here no there
Of little importance

Never say die
Don't give up hope

No bed of roses
Something difficult

No laughing matter
Something serious

Complete the following sentences with the correct idiomatic expressions.

1. He had been trying hard to build a cottage in the country. His friend, who had watched him working all day, said, _____. You should stop now and rest.
   approach the task with a lot of intensity

2. After working on a really difficult problem in mathematics, Jordan was completely exhausted and couldn't do another thing. He was _____.
   something impossibly bad

3. We tried to get the kite to fly, but we couldn't_____.
   become familiar and know how to do it

4. They won the prize, as well as a trip to Italy. The trip was_____.
   an additional benefit

5. The students did not understand what the instructor was explaining. They were _____.
   confused

6. Everyone else knew about the merger, but we were_____.
   not informed

7. After we had studied the plans for a long time, we proceeded to build our shed. By then we had it_____.
   worked out easily and well

8. When the boss told Jim that he was fired, he was upset and disappointed; it was _____.
   something serious

9. Once he graduated from college, he got a job and was soon_____ as he furthered his career.
   moving from success to sucess

10. His constant interruptions were a _____.
    very annoying

11. The innovations he suggested at the last meeting proved to be a_____.
    really easy

12. Her promotion to office manager was not an easy change for her. It proved to be the_____.
    the quiet time before a problem occurs

13. When she refused to go out on a date with him, he could_____.
    inferred meaning

14. When she later agreed to marry him, he was completely_____.
    surprised

Complete the following idiomatic expressions.

15. Uncharted_____
    trying something new
16. Under_____
    being critized
17. Up_____
    not decided
18. Walk_____
    be very careful
19. Weather_____
    get through a crisis
20. Above_____
    something done legally and correctly
21. Back_____
    in a difficult situation with few choices
22. Call_____
    stop working
23. Etched_____
    very rigid, to be followed precisely
24. Get_____
    starting a project to make progress

Select the correct meaning for each of the following idiomatic expressions.

25. Get up and go
    - (a) leave the room
    - (b) enthusiasm and energy

26. Hard act to follow
    - (a) difficult to repeat because of value
    - (b) do what has been done

27. Jump through hoops
    - (a) participate in a sport
    - (b) make great effort

28. In a fix
    - (a) repair
    - (b) problem

29. Keep your cool
    - (a) refresh yourself
    - (b) don't get excited

30. Last straw
    - (a) the final problem
    - (b) there are no straws left

31. Let the cat out of the bag
    - (a) reveal a secret
    - (b) rescue a situation

32. Make waves
    - (a) cause trouble
    - (b) agitate a pool

33. No bed of roses
    - (a) a gardening problem
    - (b) something difficult

34. Off the beaten track
    - (a) not on a path
    - (b) in a remote location

Check your answers with the answer key on page 155

Create short narrative situations and/or dialogs between friends or casual acquaintances, in which you would use idiomatic expressions to communicate what you mean.
Try to use them clearly to express the exact thoughts you have in mind.
Share your writings with a colleague and have them respond appropriately.

Use different idiomatic expressions similar to the ones shown on the chart on pp. 104 - 106 to create your situations and/or dialogs.
Examine the additional samples of idiomatic expressions on the reference chart on pp. 110 - 112

For editing services, email your writing as a WORD document to:
editessentials@aol.com

Idiomatic Expressions

No love lost
An evident dislike

No pain, no gain
Without effort there is no reward

Off the beaten track
In a remote location

Off the cuff
Without preparation

Off the record
In confidence

Off the top of your head
Without thinking

Off the wall
Something unconventional

On a roll
Moving from success to success

On good terms
A good relationship

On hold
No action taken

On ice
No action for the foreseeable future

On pins and needles
Very worried

On the ball
Well-informed

On the blink
Out of order

Pain in the neck
Very annoying

Paint yourself into a corner
Get into a difficult situation

Pass the buck
Avoid responsibility

Pass the time of day
Spend time socializing

Pay the piper
Accept the consequences

Pay through the nose
Pay a very high price

Pecking order
Order of importance and responsibility

Pep talk
A talk to build up confidence

Pie in the sky
An impractical idea

Piece of cake
Something really easy

Quick fix
An easy solution

Quiet before the storm
The quiet time before a problem occurs

Rack you brain
Think hard

Rain on your parade
To ruin someone's pleasure or plans

Rainy day
Saving for some possible problem in the future

Rather you than me
Relief that trouble doesn't fall on the speaker

Idiomatic Expressions

Raw deal
Unfair treatment

Read between the lines
Inferred meaning

Recharge your batteries
Doing something to regain energy

Recipe for disaster
A mixture of events that could be trouble

Rest on your laurels
Relying on past achievements

No rhyme or reason
Something unreasonable

Safe and sound
Nothing of harm has happened

Safe bet
There are no risks attached

Same old, same old
Nothing ever changes

Save face
Defending your reputation

Scratch the surface
Superficial knowledge

Sea change
A significant change

Second thoughts
An idea is not as good as it seemed

Second wind
Finding new energy

See eye to eye
Agree on everything

See the light
Realize the truth

See you later
Saying goodbye to a friend

Tackle an issue
Dealing with a problem

Take a raincheck
Declining an offer now which might be accepted later

Take by storm
To impress

Take for granted
To assume that something will always be there

Take it in your stride
Deal with it even though it is difficult

Take stock
Assess a situation

Take the edge off
Reduce the effect of something

Take the heat
Accept criticism or blame

Take the plunge
Commit to an action even if there is risk involved

Take your breath away
To be astonished or surprised

Take your eye off the ball
Stop concentrating

Taken aback
Surprised

Idiomatic Expressions

Uncalled for
Something unnecessary

Uncharted Waters
Trying something new

Under a cloud
Suspected of having done something wrong

Under fire
Being criticized

Under the gun
Under pressure to do something

Under your breath
To say something quietly

Up in the air
Not decided

Up the creek
In trouble

Up to scratch
Meeting the required standard

Up to speed
To be current

Upset the apple cart
Cause trouble

Vicious circle
A sequence of events that makes things worse

Waiting in the wing
Being in the background, ready to act

Wake up and smell the coffee
Pay attention

Wake-up call
A warning

Walk a fine line
Be very careful

Water over the dam
Something in the past that cannot be changed

Weather a storm
Get through a crisis

Sample Situations Using Idiomatic Expressions

Were you able to *save face* in your meeting with your boss?

It was a piece of cake. Our project is on a roll and he thinks I'm on the ball.

Rather you than me! Are you getting ready for a *rainy day*, by any chance?

I'll rack my brain to see what you mean. Do you need a pep talk?

I'm just *passing the time of day*. If I don't *get cracking*, I'll be in *a tight spot*.

It's just a vicious circle working here. I'm getting a second wind and haven't yet scratched the surface of my project.

Well, *take the plunge*, and don't *take your eye off the ball*. Don't *take your project for granted*, or you'll have to *take the heat* when your boss *waits in the wings* to *take stock* of the situation.

I don't want to upset the apple cart. Go!

Unit 17

Phrases

Phrases

Noun Phrases

A noun phrase consists of a noun and its modifiers.

The *long and winding road* was covered with snow and ice this morning.
The *road following the edge of the frozen lake* was muddy and slippery yesterday.
The *road next to the stream across the bridge* is the one we need to take.

Prepositional Phrases

A prepositional phrase consists of a preposition, and a noun or pronoun. It can contain adjectives.

On this side of the tracks there were no trees to provide shade, so the station was baking *in the blinding sun* as we entered it.
Against the side of the building there was a doorway with a curtain of bamboo beads hung *across the open door*, keeping out curious neighbors.

Appositive Phrases

An appositive phrase renames or amplifies a word that immediately precedes it.

The best daily exercise, *walking*, is also the least expensive and the easiest to do.
His goal, *to become a soccer player*, will be possible once he begins training.

Absolute Phrases

An absolute phrase does not connect to any specific word in the rest of the sentence. It modifies the whole sentence by adding information.

The season nearly over, the team was discouraged by their numerous losses.
The children played on the swings, *their faces full of delight*.

Infinitive Phrases

An infinitive phrase consists of an infinitive and modifiers or complements associated with it. Infinitive phrases can be used as adjectives, adverbs or nouns.

Her plan *to begin a child care facility* won wide acceptance among working mothers. *(adjective)*

To watch Uncle Billy tell one of his many jokes, is an entertaining experience. *(noun)*
Juan went to Europe *to get married*. *(adverb)*

Gerund Phrases

A gerund phrase acts as a noun. It is often part of a prepositional phrase.

Studying for an exam is very important.
John enjoyed *swimming in the lake* last summer.

Participial Phrases

A participial phrase always acts as an adjective. It uses the present participle *(ing)* or the past participle *(ed)*.

The stone steps on the garden walk, *cleaned in the morning*, needed to be washed again in the afternoon.

The pond, *frozen over since early December*, tempted many skaters to venture onto the dangerous ice.

Working diligently around the clock, the volunteers completed the neighborhood project in time for the holidays.

Identify the underlined phrases in each of the following sentences.

1. The midsummer breeze caused the vines <u>on the trellis</u> to sway.

   (a) prepositional phrase
   (b) participial phrase
   (c) noun phrase
   (d) gerund phrase
   (e) appositive phrase
   (f) absolute phrase
   (g) infinitive phrase

2. <u>Swinging in the park</u>, the young child laughed loudly and gleefully.

   (a) prepositional phrase
   (b) participial phrase
   (c) noun phrase
   (d) gerund phrase
   (e) appositive phrase
   (f) absolute phrase
   (g) infinitive phrase

3. The young man wanted <u>to travel to Europe</u>, but was afraid that it was going to be too expensive.

   (a) prepositional phrase
   (b) participial phrase
   (c) noun phrase
   (d) gerund phrase
   (e) appositive phrase
   (f) absolute phrase
   (g) infinitive phrase

4. <u>Excited by the country fair</u>, the children ran into the amusement park.

   (a) prepositional phrase
   (b) participial phrase
   (c) noun phrase
   (d) gerund phrase
   (e) appositive phrase
   (f) absolute phrase
   (g) infinitive phrase

5. The woman <u>standing behind the tree</u> was taking photographs of the park.

   (a) prepositional phrase
   (b) participial phrase
   (c) noun phrase
   (d) gerund phrase
   (e) appositive phrase
   (f) absolute phrase
   (g) infinitive phrase

6. <u>Winter nearly over</u>, the garden began to grow.

   (a) prepositional phrase
   (b) participial phrase
   (c) noun phrase
   (d) gerund phrase
   (e) appositive phrase
   (f) absolute phrase
   (g) infinitive phrase

7. She had never ejoyed <u>going shopping</u>, and she didn't enjoy it today.

    (a) prepositional phrase
    (b) participial phrase
    (c) noun phrase
    (d) gerund phrase
    (e) appositive phrase
    (f) absolute phrase
    (g) infinitive phrase

8. While he watched the soccer match, <u>the long-awaited contest</u>, he tapped his feet impatiently.

    (a) prepositional phrase
    (b) participial phrase
    (c) noun phrase
    (d) gerund phrase
    (e) appositive phrase
    (f) absolute phrase
    (g) infinitive phrase

Underline the participial phrases and circle the words they modify.

9. Walking steadily uphill, the hikers grew very weary.

10. The children, playing until the sun had set, finally hurried home.

11. Disappointed, the young couple walked away from the theater hand in hand.

12. The people at the picnic, worried about the approaching storm, sought shelter.

13. Blowing eerily around the house, the wind kept us awake all night.

Underline the absolute phrases in the following sentences.

14. She turned away from her friends, her manner expressing her disappointment.

15. Around the willow tree, the children ran, their shouts of laughter filling the air.

16. She watched the moon rising, her senses filled with wonder

17. A group of boys ran along the street in the early afternoon, shouting loudly, their voices shrill in the stillness, their breaths icy in the cold, their hair blowing in the wind.

18. I saw the woman sitting on the porch, her long hair unkempt and blowing in the gentle breeze, her mood ruminative and distant, the dog asleep at her feet.

19. He came back in the evening, soaked with rain, his hair and clothing drenched.

Check your answers with the answer key on page 155

Write sentences using the seven possible types of phrases.
Try to make the sentences long and interesting,
with several different images in each for the reader to enjoy.
Try to combine several sentences into a unified paragraph.

Use different phrases similar to the ones shown on the chart on p. 114
to create your sentences.
Examine the additional samples of the seven types of phrases on the reference chart on p. 118

For editing services, email your writing as a WORD document to:
editessentials@aol.com

Sample Sentences Using Various Types of Phrases

He interested me because he was so quiet and solitary and so happy, a well of good humor and contentment which overflowed at his eyes.

After reading and writing, in the forenoon, I usually bathed again in the pond, swimming across one of its coves, and washed the dust of labor from my person, or smoothed out the last wrinkle which study had made, and for the afternoon was absolutely free.

Sometimes I rambled to pine groves, standing like temples, or like fleets at sea, soft and green and shady; or to the cedar wood, where the trees, covered with blueberries, grow higher and higher, and the creeping juniper covers the ground with wreaths full of fruit.

In October I went grape picking to the river meadows, and loaded myself with clusters more precious for their beauty and fragrance than for food.

Like the water, the Walden ice, seen near at hand, has a green tint, but at a distance is beautifully blue, and you can easily tell it from the white ice of the river, or the merely greenish ice of some ponds, a quarter of a mile off.

The opening of large tracts by the ice cutters commonly causes a pond to break up earlier, for the water, agitated by the wind, even in cold weather, wears away the surrounding ice.

At length the sun's rays have attained the right angle, and warm winds blow up mist and rain and melt the snowbanks, and the sun, dispersing the mist, smiles on a checkered landscape of russet and white smoking with incense, through which the traveler picks his way from islet to islet, cheered by the music of a thousand tinkling rills and rivulets whose veins are filled with the blood of winter which they are bearing off.

The change from storm and winter to serene and mild weather, from dark and sluggish hours to bright and elastic ones, is a memorable crisis which all things proclaim.

I looked out the window, and where yesterday was cold gray ice there lay the transparent pond already calm and full of hope as in a summer evening, reflecting a summer evening sky in its bosom, though none was visible overhead.

From *Walden*
Henry David Thoreau

Unit 18

Writing Points

Writing Points

Planning an Essay

Determining the General & Specific Purpose of the Essay

Expressing yourself
Informing readers
Persuading readers

Tone is the attitude towards the topic and/or the reader. The tone can be casual or formal, informative or lecturing, sarcastic and condescending, or understanding.

Understanding the Audience Being Addressed

Consider what the reader already knows
Decide what new information would be relevant to the reader
Determine what subject the reader would care about
Identify which ideas the reader would not accept

Exploring the Subject & Developing Support Getting Ideas

Freewriting
Clustering
Brainstorming
Listing

Writing a Topic Sentence

The topic sentence announces and summarizes the subject, introducing the information

Writing a Thesis Statement

The thesis statement describes the purpose of the essay and what it will prove or discuss about the subject

Planning the Organization

Introductory paragraph
Body paragraph 1
Body paragraph 2
Body paragraph 3
Concluding paragraph

Outlining an Essay

I. **Introduction**

   Thesis statement_____

II. **Body Paragraph 1**

   Opening sentence_____
   Detail 1_____
   Detail 2_____
   Detail 3_____
   Concluding sentence_____

III. **Body Paragraph 2**

   Transition/Opening sentence_____
   Detail 1_____
   Detail 2_____
   Detail 3_____
   Concluding sentence_____

IV. **Body Paragraph 3**

   Transition/Opening sentence_____
   Detail 1_____
   Detail 2_____
   Detail 3_____
   Concluding sentence_____

V. **Conclusion**

   Reconfirmation of thesis_____

Drafting an Essay

Types of Topic Sentences

The direct approach
There are many concepts of liberty.
The question
What is the role of liberty in daily life?
The nutshell
Liberty is the free exercise of individual choice.
Addressing the reader
Consider the concept of freedom in your own life.
Connecting to the previous paragraph
If we consider these aspects, we will understand the issue.
The alert
There is imminent danger of losing personal freedom.

Revising an Essay

Basic standard 1
Check that the general purpose of the essay is clearly described

Basic standard 2
Check that all the details clearly support the stated thesis

Basic standard 3
Analyze the overall organization of the essay to be sure the meaning is clear

Basic standard 4
Analyze the general style for cohesiveness and structural accuracy

Unit 19

Essay Structure

Essay Structure

Defining an Essay

An essay is a short written composition on one topic that expresses the views of the writer.

Organizing an Essay

An essay is made up of at least five paragraphs organized into three basic parts

Introduction
Body
Conclusion

Writing an Introduction

The introduction gives background information
It presents the topic which is the primary subject of the essay
It includes a thesis statement, which is the writer's ideas on the topic

Topic sentence
This is the subject of the essay

Thesis statement
This is the writer's opinion on the subject

Understanding the Body

The body explains and supports the thesis statement,
by giving examples and stating arguments.

Understanding the Conclusion

The conclusion restates the thesis, which is the writer's main point
It summarizes, repeating introductory ideas, makes a prediction, gives advice or makes a suggestion.

Essay Outline

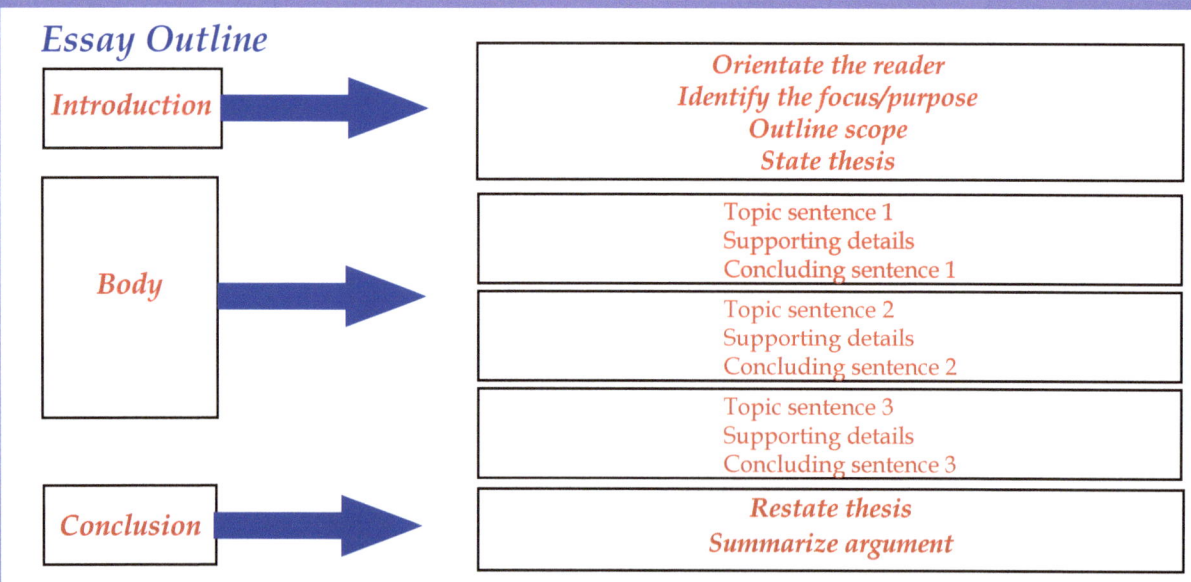

Essay Format

Capture Attention
Thesis
Three Supporting Ideas/Areas of Focus

Supporting Idea 1

- Topic Sentence
- Examples/Details

1._____

2._____

3._____

Conclusion/Transition
Focused Statement

Supporting Idea 2

- Topic Sentence
- Examples/Details

1._____

2._____

3._____

Conclusion/Transition
Focused Statement

Supporting Idea 3

- Topic Sentence
- Examples/Details

1._____

2._____

3._____

Conclusion/Transition
Focused Statement

Restate Thesis
Restate General Supporting Ideas
Powerful Conclusion or Statement of Significance

	Sample Outline for Definition Essay
Title	*Purpose and Experience in Henry David Thoreau's* Walden
Introductory Paragraph Attention Getter Thesis Statement Areas of Focus Concluding Statement	"I went to the woods because I wished to live deliberately…" Description of reasons for life changes • Responses to life changes • Occupations in changed circumstances • Experience of the seasons Summary of purpose
Body Paragraph 1 Topic Sentence Examples/Details Concluding Statement	Responses to life changes Discussion of responses • Economy • Housing • Pastimes Summary of responses
Body Paragraph 2 Topic Sentence Examples/Details Concluding Statement	Occupations in changed circumstances Discussion of occupations • Environment • People • Animals Summary of occupations
Body Paragraph 3 Topic Sentence Examples/Details Concluding Statement	Experience of the seasons Discussion of experiences • Autumn • Winter • Spring Summary of experiences
Concluding Paragraph Thesis Restatement Topic Sentence Restatement of Supporting Ideas Concluding Sentence with a prediction, suggestion or advice	Purpose of going to the woods Reason for change • Adaptation to changed circumstances • Occupations in changed circumstances • Experiences of the seasons Summarize purpose

Unit 20

Essay Outlines & Sample Essays

Sentences in green are the topic sentences or thesis statements of each paragraph

Transitions are indicated in blue

Notes describing the content of each paragraph are in red

Narrative Essay

- A narrative essay tells a story in chronological order, with thoughts and feelings that are important to the writer

- It is written from a personal perspective to teach the reader a lesson based on a common human experience.

- The story can be an anecdote communicating an insight.

- It can be a real experience that stresses a particular point.

- It can be a piece of fiction with an introduction, a plot, characters, a setting and a conclusion or climax.

- The action should begin immediately with descriptive language to convey specific emotions and impressions to the reader.

- The language should be concrete so that the reader can visualize the actions clearly.

Essay Outline

Introductory Paragraph
Topic Sentence_____
Thesis Statement_____

Body Paragraph 1
Event 1_____
_____

Body Paragraph 2
Event 2_____
_____

Body Paragraph 3
Event 3_____
_____

Concluding Paragrah
Concluding Statement (*summarizes and repeats introductory ideas, makes a prediction, gives advice, makes a suggestion*)
_____
_____

Steps in Writing a Narrative Essay

Identify the experience you want to relate from the list of prompts below.
Identify the reasons this experience is significant.
Do free writing about the recollections of the experience.
Arrange your ideas in an outline, as shown on the previous page.

Transitions for Narrative Essays

first	finally	then	consequently
at first	before	suddenly	ultimately
second	earlier	eventually	by the time
third	when	immediately	at the time
next	as	meanwhile	prior to that
later	as soon as	now	after
two hours later	by this time	until	concurrently
later on	at the same time	soon	simultaneously

Topic Possibilities

An interesting event	A perfect day
The summary of a book/movie	A significant decision
A dismal day	A family story
A difficult choice	A frightening situation
A time of self-doubt	A success/failure
A lesson you learned	A happy moment
An embarrassing situation	A surprise
A moment of understanding	A special insight
An amusing story	A good-luck story
A life-changing event	A memory
Achieving a goal	A childhood event
A good/bad day	A significant journey

Assessment for Narrative Essays

Does the **first paragraph** introduce the important people and places?
Does the **thesis statement** state the writer's purpose?
Are the **events** arranged in order of occurrence?

Are there enough **details** to make the narrative interesting?
Do the **transitional words & phrases** help clarify the sequence of events?
Does the **conclusion** explain why this story was told?

Model Narrative Essay

Topic/thesis statements
Transitions
Paragraph descriptions

May, 1952

    It was spring in Germany, May to be exact, with its burst of blooming trees and bouquets of flowers. It was a most beautiful and memorable May, one that would be forever engraved on the memory of the nine-year-old who saw this particular spring effulgence for the last time. She knew that this was so without having been told specifically and her eyes and mind filled with the quiet foreboding of loss and change, of leaving the familiar and trusted, to venture into the larger realm of the unknown and unknowable. It seemed that this was the last time the sun shone. *Setting the scene of contrast, initiating intimations of loss and change in a thesis statement that reveals aspects of negative things to come.*

    She had waved one last time to her weeping grandparents *that morning*, as the bus rumbled away from the small farming village in which she had spent the greater part of her conscious life. It was to be an adventure, but the sense of farewell suddenly became clear. It was imprinted on her mind on the long train journey north to the harbor, the train journey on which, she, who normally relished the clatter of train wheels and the whooshing of wind through trees, remembered not a thing, so preoccupied was her mind with strange foreboding. Her memory of that trip was a black, blank slate. *Detail of presentiments of departure and change in emotional state on leaving home and facing an unsure future.*

    That next evening is blurred in her memory, filled with shadowy grey images and tinged with loss. Noone seemed to speak much in the harbor city on the night before the ship was to depart for the new world. She went to see the dark hulk of the ship in the dark, overhung slip, and felt her safety and security slip from her. The ship was dark, the harbor was dark, and her heart was dark with loss and foreboding. *Detail of emotions prior to departure and loss of the familiar world on contemplating the change agent - the ship and the enormous sea that was to be crossed, separating the known world from the unknown and possibly dangerous one.*

    By this time, she knew that this ancient vessel was to transport her to a new and unknown world, across an ocean never seen and never-ending, docking first in Southampton - the enemy in the eyes of a nine-year-old who had experienced the recent ravages of war between her country and this one. Then began the seemingly endless journey across the great expanse of the North Atlantic, to the snow- and ice-encrusted far reaches of Labrador at the mouth of the great St. Lawrence River in Canada. *Details of the transition from the known and familiar to the almost threatening aspect of the new world to be inhabited without recourse.*

    She *finally* understood fully what had happened to her life; how she had exchanged a blissful spring for this frozen wasteland; how she had given up the familiar and how she had lost the comforts of home and family; how she had exchanged the soft beauty of her homeland for this harsh and unyielding icy mass. Her loss could not have been more evident. The changes she had embarked upon could not have been more stark and devastating. *Conclusion reemphasizing the changes in living circumstances and the writer's responses to it, reemphasizing the negative portends of the opening paragraph.*

Descriptive Essay

- A descriptive essay describes a person, object, event, situation or experience so that the reader can accurately visualize it.

- It uses all the senses to describe the subject so that a clear visual image is created for the reader.

- The essay allows a great deal of creative freedom to paint a vivid and moving image in the mind of the reader.

- It uses vivid language that embellishes the subject with emotionally tinged senses.

- It is important to clearly describe the emotions and feelings that relate to the topic.

- Good descriptive essays evoke strong appreciation and familiarity in the reader.

- Even though the essay is filled with emotional content, it still needs to be sufficiently organized to avoid rambling, disconnected thoughts.

Essay Outline

Introductory Paragraph
Topic Sentence_____
Thesis Statement_____

Body Paragraph 1
Detail 1_____
_____

Body Paragraph 2
Detail 2_____
_____

Body Paragraph 3
Detail 3_____
_____

Concluding Paragraph
Concluding Statement *(summarizes and repeats introductory ideas, makes a prediction, gives advice, makes a suggestion)*
_____
_____

Steps in Writing a Descriptive Essay

Identify the person, object, event, situation or experience you want to relate from the list of prompts below.
Identify the important aspects of the subject & list the sensory details you want to include.
Do free writing about the emotions and feelings inspired by the subject.

Transitions for Descriptive Essays

above	beyond	after all	in the long run
below	on the other side	in essence	to sum up
between	inside	truly	next to
in front of	outside	in contrast	beside
in back of	next to	likewise	opposite
on one side	for instance	similarly	although
nearby	in other words	during	even so
over	above all	all in all	therefore

Topic Possibilities

A favorite place to be	A sunrise/sunset
A comfortable experience	A tropical storm
A preferred place to live	A special landscape
A friend	My dream car
A valued possession	A memorable trip
A favorite pet	A difficult course
A favorite place to visit	An important job
An admired person	A difficult encounter
A family member	A wrong choice
A work of art	A fortunate decision
A useful object	A special child
A special building	A remarkable relationship

Assessment for Descriptive Essays

Does the introduction **identify the subject** clearly?
Does the first paragraph give an **impression of the writer's feelings** about the subject?
Does the essay present a vivid picture with **meaningful descriptive language**?

Do the **details** and language support the impression the writer is trying to convey?
Do the **transitional words & phrases** move smoothly from one section to the next?
Does the conclusion reinforce the **impression** the writer is trying to create?

Model Descriptive Essay

Espagna

■ Topic/thesis statements
■ Transitions
■ Paragraph descriptions

It was a journey that imprinted itself on my memory and on my heart. Spain had always fascinated me in that it was so geographically and culturally divergent from the Europe and Northeast US I had known all my life. I had become enamored of Spanish music and art, and I valued Spain's history and its important role at the apex of its power in the world. It seemed a romantic and promising place, and I eagerly planned for my visit, not realizing that I would be forever enthralled by its magic. *Introduction stating reasons for the interest in exploring Spain.*

My most significant impressions, *from least significant to most memorable*, begin in Seville, where my journey of emotional discovery started. After driving through southern Spain's desert landscape, in which the wind itself was hot, I crossed the river into Seville and was immediately captivated. Here was a culture I had not witnessed before, with a lifestyle totally different from any I had yet experienced. Color and light, rest and repast, history and the present, all mingled in a magical mixture that delighted the eyes and the senses, and was unforgettable. *Explanation and details about the different experience one of the cities visited provided.*

Cordoba, *on the other hand,* provided serious contemplation of philosophers, artisans and the long-ago Moorish influence. The great mosque, dim in reverence, with carefully spaced columns, expressed the importance of the individual and the anonymous and personal prayer ritual of the muslim faith. The windows of historical artisans below street level, viewed from above as one walked past, attested to Cordoba's endemic art and sense of historical preservation. In the evening, I dined on a rooftop terrace with the sounds of Spanish guitar music wafting through the cooling night air. I was transported to another time and place, and felt completely at home and at peace. *Explanation and details about the importance of Cordoba to the writer's sensibilities.*

Beyond this experience of beauty was the Alhambra in Granada. I stayed in a converted nunnery and experienced the Spanish night falling over the city as I walked the hillside gardens, filled with the gentle splashing sounds of fountains. The decorated interiors stunned me to silent contemplation. Their intricacy attested to the skill and love of ornament of a long-forgotten society that had ruled southern Spain hundreds of years before. *Explanation and details of man-made beauty and its effect on the viewer.*

Cradled in the visual beauty of the historical monuments, and the remembrance of, and reverence for, the past in artisanship, Andalusia provides the visitor with an ineffable emotional experience that transcends simple everyday appreciation and becomes a soul-stirring paen to a culture revealed in intricate beauty and treasure. It was an unforgettable experience to become a part of these three great cities for even a short time and to succumb to their magical touch. I saw other sights on this trip, such as the southern coastline, but I barely remember these scenes, so captivated was I by the soul of Spain as revealed in its Moorish past. *Explanation and details of the general effect of Moorish Spain on modern-day visitors.*

Comparison/Contrast Essay

- ❖ Comparison/contrast essays discuss either the similarities or differences, or both, of two objects, places, ways of life, or issues, of a subject familiar to the writer.

- ❖ The topic sentence should clarify whether the essay will describe similarities or differences, or both, of two different things.

- ❖ The things discussed can have totally different characteristics, or they can be fit into the same category. The essay can include an argument or evaluation.

- ❖ The essay should point out meaningful similarities or differences, so that the reader looks at things in a new way.

Essay Outline for Subject-by-Subject Comparisons

Introductory Paragraph
Topic Sentence_____
Thesis Statement_____

Body Paragraph 1
Subject 1_____
_____

Point 1_____
_____

Point 2_____
_____

Point 3_____
_____

Body Paragraph 2
Subject 2_____
_____

Point 1_____
_____

Point 2_____
_____

Point 3_____
_____

Concluding Paragraph
Concluding Statement *(summarizes and repeats introductory ideas, makes a prediction, gives advice, makes a suggestion)*
_____
_____

Essay Outline for Point-by-Point Comparisons

Introductory Paragraph
Topic Sentence_____
Thesis Statement_____

Body Paragraph 1
Point 1_____
_____

Subject 1_____
_____

Subject 2_____
_____

Body Paragraph 2
Point 2_____
_____

Subject 1_____
_____

Subject 2_____
_____

Body Paragraph 3
Point 3_____
_____

Subject 1_____
_____

Subject 2_____
_____

Concluding Paragraph
Concluding Statement *(summarizes and repeats inroductory ideas, makes a prediction, gives advice, makes a ggestion)*
_____
_____

Similarities Commonalities Differences

Steps in Writing a Comparison/Contrast Essay

Select a theme from the list of prompts below.
Prepare a diagram or a list of the characteristics of both aspects of the topic you have chosen.
Determine the similarities and differences, as well as the things the subjects have in common.
Do free writing on the theme and arrange your ideas in an outline, as shown on the previous page.

Transitions for Comparison/Contrast Essays

even though	another difference	likewise	at the same time
although	one similarity	in comparison	even so
though	another similarity	but	in the same way
however	on the one hand	whereas	respectively
in contrast	on the other hand	instead	accordingly
nevertheless	similarly	for example	in any case
on the contrary	like	for instance	on the whole
one difference	unlike	as an illustration	to sum up

Topic Possibilities

A movie and a book	Traveling alone or with friends
Being married or single	Major courses & electives
City or country living	Two styles of music
Historical & contemporary attitudes	Two different electronic devices
Study at home or abroad	Two styles of architecture
Formal or cottage gardens	Two cities
Two countries	Two modes of travel
Cars	Guided tours or individual travel
Lifestyle activities	Two career choices
Living along or living with someone	Internet or on-site classes
Two different historical periods	Two different ideas
Two famous people	Two different futures

Assessment for Comparison/Contrast Essays

Does the introduction clearly **identify the two subjects** to be compared/contrasted?
Does the thesis statement make it clear whether **similarities, differences, or both**, will be discussed?
Are the **supporting details** related to the theme?

Are the **topic sentences** of each paragraph clearly related to the points being discussed?
Do the **transitional words & phrases** move smoothly from one point to the next?
Does the **conclusion focus** clearly on the two subjects being compared/contrasted?

Model Comparison and Contrast Essay

■ *Topic/thesis statements*
■ *Transitions*
■ *Paragraph descriptions*

City or Suburb?

There is hardly any argument in recent days about the preferred place to live, whether in a city or in a suburb. In great old cities like New York, for example, the suburbs surround the island of Manhattan and there is a clear cut-off point for the location of suburbs. In other cities, those not surrounded by water on all sides, the city forms a core from which tentacles of outlying places to live reach out and stretch for many miles. While these arrangements differ from locality to locality, there are certain points of comparison and contrast that can be readily made. *Introduction to the idea that points of similarity and difference exist between cities and suburbs.*

When anyone discuses differences and similarities in urban and suburban living, the matter of convenience immediately arises. There is no doubt that cities provide certain geographical advantages for urban residents, such as ease of access to work and entertainment venues. However, unless the urbanite owns a car, convenience can easily become a form of entrapment, in that it is difficult to escape the physical boundaries of the city. In this day and age, the suburbs offer as many, if not more, conveniences, and these are readily accessed by car, with the added ease of parking, which is not available to city dwellers. *Describing the differences in city and suburban access to work and entertainment facilities.*

The availability of shopping, recreational, cultural and educational facilities is another difference between urban and suburban life. Once upon a time, when cities were the principle places of residence, these facilities were only available there, whereas, for the past fifty years, more and more such facilities have become available in communities surrounding the central town. Even cultural and sporting events, while largely confined to cities, have often been held away from the large urban centers for ease of access. The cities, in some respects, are being abandoned for the suburbs, where various facilities are beginning to predominate due to the need to provide access to families with children. *Describing the availability of many facilities in the suburbs as opposed to the cities.*

On the other hand, if a resident strives for anonymity and privacy, cities continue to amply supply these features. The concept of being left alone in a city to pursue one's work and lifestyle is often decried as dehumanizing, even though this anonymity is preferred over the more intrusive, neighborly manners in suburban enclaves. There, neighbors are aware of each other and can prove to be helpful, whereas it has been demonstrated that the isolation of city residents can prove deadly to someone in genuine difficulties. Anonymity deadens humanity, but can provide a protective barrier to unwelcome encroachments. *Describing the differences in privacy concerns between cities and suburbs.*

Although the choice of a place to live depends on personal preference, cities continue to lose residents. As a result, they decay, as families with children move to the safer and more accessible suburbs to enjoy the suburbs' growing features. While single, younger people value the perceived convenience and sophistication of the city, the suburban environment seems to appeal more to people who have already experienced the more youthful lifestyle and are ready to settle for greater ease and community. *Summary of perceptions regarding urban and suburban lifestyles.*

Persuasive Essay

- ❖ A persuasive or argument essay tries to convince a reader to acccept the writer's opinion on a particular issue.

- ❖ The argument is supported by actual evidence, or facts, statistics or valid reasoning.

- ❖ The thesis statement clearly describes the topic, the proposed argument, and the opinion of the writer.

- ❖ The writer needs to make a strong claim, with a strong position.

- ❖ The writer needs to communicte precisely what should happen in the particular case, using passionate language.

- ❖ Opposing arguments need to be soundly defeated.

Essay Outline

Introductory Paragraph
Topic Sentence_____
Thesis Statement_____

Body Paragraph 1
Point 1_____
_____
Point 2_____
_____
Point 3_____
_____

Body Paragraph 2
Opposing Argument 1_____
_____

Body Paragraph 3
Opposing Argument 2_____
_____

Concluding Paragraph
Concluding Statement (*summarizes and repeats introductory ideas, makes a prediction, gives advice, makes a suggestion*)
_____
_____

Steps in Writing a Persuasive Essay

Choose an idea you feel strongly about from the list of prompts below.
Make a list of the evidence and facts that support the argument you propose to make.
List the supporting reasons for your opinion on the issue.
Organize the facts and reasons into a clear outline as shown on the previous page.

Transitions for Persuasive Essays

even though	admittedly	above all	in contrast
although	after all	after all	in the same way
though	because	certainly	otherwise
however	despite	indeed	therefore
in contrast	in fact	in essence	for the most part
nevertheless	in spite of	in particular	typically
on the contrary	for example	as a result	usually
accordingly	for instance	at the same time	consequently

Topic Possibilities

Environmental concerns	Differing philosophies
The value of education	How to succeed
The role of the arts	Addiction
Political concepts	Narcissism
Lifestyles	Relationships
Taxation	Political upheavals
Subjects of study	Economic realities
Immigration	Technology
Work and leisure	Historical realities
Study methods	War & peace
The individual & the group	Human aspirations
Religious beliefs	Psychological perspectives

Assessment for Persuasive Essays

Does the introduction clearly state the **writer's opinion**?
Does the issue have two **clearly debatable** sides?
Does the argument **convince** a reader who does not agree with the premise?

Is the opposing argument adequately **refuted** by the writer's arguments?
Is there enough **evidence** to support the points made?
Does the evidence presented lead to a **logical conclusion**?

Model Persuasive Essay

Individual Liberty and Government Dictates

Topic/thesis statements
Transitions
Paragraph descriptions

There are two views of human nature. One view states that human nature is basically flawed and therefore needs to be controlled by a superior gifted elite or else chaos will result. The other viewpoint holds that mankind is basically good and capable and can be entrusted with his own life and that of others within the social network. One opinion leads to enslavement, the other to liberty. These conflicting world views cause all the difficulties between governments and the governed. *Statement of problem and its ramifications.*

Admittedly, it is the will to power of the few that inhibits the free will of the many. Yet the drive to power that afflicts a small segment of humankind has enormous potential to assert itself through elected offices in every country of the world. Thus is born the result of malignant narcissism. Accordingly, those whose self-centered will knows no boundary must align themselves with dictatorial means in order to exert more and more control over ever larger segments of humanity. Nothing but ultimate control satisfies their insatiable craving to hold others hostage to their will. Conflict consequently erupts among the suppressed. Many lose their lives or their physical freedoms as they struggle against the oppression of the narcissist. *Explaining the difference between those who need power and those who suffer its consequences.*

Supporters of control mechanisms, *in fact*, claim that only they know best and that the common people don't have the knowledge or experience to govern themselves in a manner considered suitable by the ruling elites. Only the enlightened supervisors have sufficient standing and expertise to tell others how to live and how to respond to the rulers' dictates. These ruling oligarchies consider themselves the anointed guides of society and human interaction. *Introduction of counter-arguments, explaining the self-reflective attitudes of those who seek to control.*

In addition, it is postulated that only certain enlightened people can control the evil proclivities of mankind, so that man's relationship to man is strengthened and we develop into a more just and fair society. These rulers believe that life and people are inherently unjust and selfish, and that the rule of law must be applied by enlightened guides to control these tendencies. *Additional utopian argument against individual freedom.*

In conclusion, it is debatable whether these tendencies to control are due to psychotic perceptions of self-adulation and aggrandizement, or to the sociopathic sensation of inferiority. Whatever its motivation and impetus, the end result is the destruction of the soul of others as they dance to the manipulations of the psychologically disturbed. Mankind was born for individual freedom, obeying a free will and able to tolerate only a minor amount of oppression, before, like water behind a dam, it breaks free of all restraints and floods the entire landscape, irrespective of whose land it is - the oppressor's or that of the oppressed. *Counter-argument to explain the inevitable results of oppression.*

Definition Essays

- A definition essay explains a particular opinion on a subject, a term, or a concept whose exact significance can be disputed.

- The formal meaning of the topic or word can be based on the generally accepted definition, whether from a dictionary, or from a universally accepted source.

- The thesis statement clearly states the author's purpose in writing the essay, and begins the process of defining that idea from the author's perspective.

- Examples and illustrations are purposefully used to define the concept clearly.

- Opposing arguments are explained and refuted logically to defend the writer's position.

Essay Outline
Option 1

Introductory Paragraph
Topic Sentence_____
Thesis Statement_____

Body Paragraph 1
Example 1_____
_____
Example 2_____
_____
Example 3_____
_____

Body Paragraph 2
Opposing Argument 1_____
_____

Body Paragraph 3
Opposing Argument 2_____
_____

Concluding Paragraph
Concluding Statement (*summarizes and repeats introductory ideas, makes a prediction, gives advice, makes a suggestion*)
_____
_____

Essay Outline
Option 2

Introductory Paragraph
Topic Sentence_____
Thesis Statement_____

Body Paragraph 1
Description_____
_____

Body Paragraph 1
Example_____

Body Paragraph 3
Comparison/contrast_____

Concluding Paragraph
Concluding Statement (*summarizes and repeats introductory ideas, makes a prediction, gives advice, makes a suggestion*)
_____
_____

Sample Concepts for Definitions Essays

The finest qualities of our nature, like the bloom on fruits, can be preserved only by the most delicate handling. Yet we do not treat ourselves nor one another thus tenderly.

In any weather, at any hour of the day or night, I have been anxious to improve the nick of time, and notch it on my stick too; to stand on the meeting of two eternities, the past and the future, which is precisely the present moment; to toe that line.

Why should we be in such desperate haste to succeed and in such desperate enterprises? If a man does not keep pace with his companions, perhaps it is because he hears a different drummer. Let him step to the music which he hears, however measured or far away.

The light which puts out our eyes is darkness to us. Only that day dawns to which we are awake. There is more day to dawn. The sun is but a morning star.

I went to the woods because I wished to live deliberately, to front only the essential facts of life, and see if I could not learn what it had to teach, and not, when I came to die, discover that I had not lived.

Henry David Thoreau, **Walden**

Steps in Writing a Definition Essay

Choose a concept that appeals to you from the list of prompts below.
Summarize the possibilities in the ideas contained in the topic suggestion.
Paraphrase the thoughts using descriptive language.
Do free writing to express your own responses to the topic.

Transitions for Definition Essays

not only	for example	the importance of	for instance
but also	as shown	clearly	as an illustration
depending on	like	it seems that	in essence
defined as	another way	according to	in particular
while	the purpose of	in most cases	at the same time
also	the fact that	obviously	in the same way
in particular	the effect of	certainly	on the whole
one characteristic	the aim of	absolutely	respectively

Topic Possibilities

Upward mobility	Life & death
Wealth	Pain
Competition	Suffering
Security	Bliss
Happiness	Contentment
Peer pressure	Courage
Success	Knowledge
Procrastination	Wisdom
Courage	Foolishness
Home	Love
Family	Remembrance
Friends	Loss

Assessment for Definition Essays

Does the writer include a **formal definition** of the concept?
Does the thesis statement explain the **reason for writing** the essay?
Are all the details and examples **related** to the subject?

Is the basic idea **broad** enough to be of interest to the reader?
Has the writer included intensive **descriptive** language?
Is the essay development **meaningful** and persuasive?

Model Definition Essay

Topic/thesis statements
Transitions
Paragraph descriptions

The Experienced Life

If a man does not keep pace with his companions, perhaps it is because he hears a different drummer. Let him step to the music which he hears, however measured or far away.
Henry David Thoreau, **Walden**

Approximately one hundred fifty years ago, a reclusive man left the comforts of civilization to build himself a cabin in the woods and to grow his own food. During the time he lived there, he allowed himself to be aware of the remarkable changes in the seasons and the miraculous insights these changes brought him, as he lived a life of self-determination and peace. *Explanation of what the author of the quote did to enhance his own life.*

He felt *specifically* that the sanctity of being alone, of hearing his own inner voice, created strength in him to consider his own ways and wishes. Solitude imparted immense awareness as he observed both subtle and profound changes in nature around him. The anxiety-ridden ways of the world became unimportant; the significance of the stressful rush to achieve what success was possible in the infinitely minuscule moment, receded, and he became grounded in his own internal reality. *The initial results of his experiment in living a solitary life, surrounded by the natural world.*

In particular, he explains that not everyone craves the same results for his striving. Each individual possesses a level of self-determination which compels and controls his actions and responses. Everyone's perceptions of objective and subjective reality differ, and everyone's responses are unique to the extent that perceptions are clarified and understood in a new way. One man's perceptions are influenced by his mental and emotional development processes and by his individual experiences in life, and the concomitant self-assurance and pride they have provided through the course of his life experience. *Beginning explanation of self-determination and exploration.*

One characteristic of the directed meaning of Thoreau's statement is that every person needs to be an individual, dependent only on his own perceptions and unique responses to the experiences that have attended the progress of his life. It is due to these unique perceptions of experience that the person as individual is created, responsible only to himself, while retaining loyalty to the original interpretations of experience that animate his psyche. *Details of further individuation, as the person becomes more and more self-motivated and independent.*

In addition, Thoreau admonishes each person to follow his own true perceptions, thereby gaining strength to follow his own path, no matter how others are dealing with interpretations of their own individual experiences. Even though intimations of truth and reality may seen faint and barely perceived, each person needs to create his own unique patterns of living. In this process, Thoreau led the way, following his own instincts in choosing a life of self-determination and understanding. *Concluding thoughts summarizing how solitude and independence lead to individuality.*

Exemplification Essay

- An exemplification essay investigates an idea using specific examples from different sources of information.

- The essay evaluates the evidence clearly and logically, using appropriate details and examples.

- The thesis statement explains how the writer will deal with the concept and the various sources of information.

- The supporting examples are arranged from least important to most important, explaining the stratification clearly.

- The purpose of the essay is to make a lasting impression on the reader.

Essay Outline

Introductory Paragraph
Topic Sentence_____
Thesis Statement_____

Body Paragraph 1
Example 1_____
_____
Example 2_____
_____

Body Paragraph 2
Example 3_____
_____

Body Paragraph 3
Opposing Argument 1_____
_____
Opposing Argument 2_____
_____

Concluding Paragraph
Concluding Statement (*summarizes and repeats introductory ideas makes a prediction, gives advice, makes a suggestion*)
_____

Steps in Writing an Exemplification Essay

Choose a topic that you understand clearly from the prompts below and investigate it.
Select various resources from which to get your information.
List the ideas you got from your research and the various sources.
Organize your ideas into a clear outline as on the previous page.

Transitions for Exemplification Essays

also	furthermore	in other words	otherwise
for example	another example	above all	similarly
moreover	the next example	after all	finally
the best	first	certainly	respectively
besides	in addition	in particular	accordingly
for instance	additionally	as a result	in brief
one example	specifically	in essence	in conclusion
finally	ordinarily	consequently	to sum up

Topic Possibilities

Extreme sports	Winning & losing
Word Cup soccer	Travel
Politics	Historical events
Rules of behavior	Technological inventions
Eradication of diseases	Personality
Language learning	Psychological profiles
Advertising	Power
Education theories	Success
Raising a family	Peacefulness
Building a business	Contentment
Leaving home	Civilization
Making friends	Human development

Assessment for Exemplification Essays

*Does the introduction express a **clear idea** of what the essay will discuss?*
*Does the thesis statement clearly reveal the **purpose** of the essay?*
*Do the examples adequately **support** the ideas being discussed?*

*Are there enough details to make the concept clear and **understandable**?*
*Has the writer included clearly **persuasive** language?*
*Does the essay contribute to a **new** way of thinking on the topic?*

🟩 *Topic/thesis statements*
🟦 *Transitions*
🟧 *Paragraph descriptions*

Model Exemplification Essay

Varying Theories of Education

Theories of appropriate ways of educating the young have continually changed since it became understood that education had value. At one time in human history, only the elite, either wealthy or gifted, were accorded the privilege of being educated. It is interesting to trace the evolution of universal education from that time to this, in which not only rights to basic education are accorded everyone, but also, the acquisition of more advanced degrees is encouraged. *Introduction to how education developed over the centuries.*

In feudal society, *for example,* basic survival skills were passed on to children by the extended family. Guilds existed to pass on specialized skills through an apprenticeship system. Basic literacy was reserved for the elite through religious schools, and was designed to showcase personal wealth, and to maintain a posture of authority. In prehistoric times, before writing, knowledge was transmitted orally by the family through stories. By 1100, in Europe, cathedral schools had been established and the first universities were founded. In 1760, Germany produced the first comprehensive theory of teaching methods. During the Industrial Revolution, the progress toward universal child education, begun previously, slowed, due to the need for children to work in factories. One example of the development of universal education is the Greek and Roman model, in which all education was private and a basic curriculum was established. *Explanatory references to early modes of education.*

By the 19th century, *moreover,* universal elementary education, focused on reading, writing and arithmetic, was designed to inculcate orderly political behavior. Thus began a century of social experimentation in the use of education to mold the ideal citizen. In Russia, boarding schools were established to "build a new race of men". In the US, John Dewey believed that education should help the person reach his full potential for use to the greater good. *Introduction to social engineering through education.*

Besides teaching basic competencies, universal education became the primary vehicle for personality manipulation. The freedoms of a cohesive and flowing curriculum structure based on student interest was developed in the British Primary School method and in the Reggio Emilia project in Italy. None of the prevailing ideas of freedom to follow one's own interests has resulted in a superbly educated or happier person. In fact, self-determination has eroded self-discipline and self-discovery has vitiated the willingness to learn from any source. *Introduction of problems associated with individualized educational methods.*

Furthermore, there is no singular solution to the proper development of the citizen. To some educators, the lack of concrete knowledge and skills is a detriment to gaining of skills required for work and a satisfactory life of continued learning. For some, the social manipulation of human beings through selected types of propaganda is extremely disturbing. One can only hope that, by having access to continuing educational opportunities, a student can discover his own correct pathway through life. *Introduction of a contrary opinion, critical of contemporary methods of educating.*

Cause & Effect Essay

- ❖ A cause and effect essay helps readers understand why something happened or how one event or action led to another.

- ❖ The topic generally deals with a major event, either in the the writer's own life, or in a historical context.

- ❖ The topic sentence briefly mentions what took place and why, identifying patterns and outlining the reasons things turned out as they did.

- ❖ The essay clearly traces each result to a specific cause, examining what happened in relationship to the event that precipitated it.

- ❖ The essay discusses the behaviors and attitudes influencing the event, and the cultural responses to it.

- ❖ The essay should include specific descriptive details to create an effect of reality for the reader.

Essay Outline

Introductory Paragraph

Topic Sentence_____
Thesis Statement_____

Body Paragraph 1
Cause/Effect 1_____
_____

Body Paragraph 2
Cause/Effect 2_____
_____

Body Paragraph 3
Cause/Effect 3_____
_____

Concluding Paragraph
Concluding Statement *(summarizes and repeats introductory ideas, makes a prediction, gives advice, makes a suggestion)*
_____
_____

Steps in Writing a Cause & Effect Essay

*Choose a topic that interests you from the list below and identify the main idea.
Make a chart of events related to the subject and write down the results of each event.
Categorize each cause and effect according to behaviors, attitudes and emotions.
Create an outline of your ideas as shown on the previous page.*

Transitions for Cause & Effect Essays

accordingly	for this reason	therefore	altogether
as a result	so	thus	as a result
for	the main reason	in other words	in the event that
since	the strongest effect	as an example	at the same time
the first effect	another effect	above all	in the same way
the last cause	consequently	after all	similarly
another cause	moreover	in essence	accordingly
because	the primary cause	in particular	in any case

Topic Possibilities

Lack of a degree	Interviewing for a new position
Changing jobs	Writing a book
Moving to another country	Joining a club
Getting married	Traveling
Political upheaval	A storm
Elections	A disaster
War	A historical event
Having a child	A person from history
Losing a friend	A fairy tale
Gaining a friend	A folktale
Graduating	A memoir
Growing up	An adventure

Assessment for Cause & Effect Essays

Does the introduction provide a **clear overview** of the causes and effects?
Does the thesis statement indicate the **specific** causes and effects?
Are all the **details** included that are required for clear understanding?

Is the writing clear and straightforward, **communicating** effectively?
Is the language **succinct** and to the point to help the reader understand?
Are the causes and effects clearly **related** and logically presented?

Model Cause and Effect Essay

The Job Change Conundrum

All the years of his life he had preferred solitude to society. In his best moments, he had studied alone, planned his own development by himself, and eschewed the influence of his peers and his mentors. He had relished the time alone and the time spent in solitary thinking, uninhibited by considerations of community or communcal responsibilities. In this way, he had prepared himself for a career that spoke to his proclivities. *Introduction of problem.*

For this reason, he had accepted a position in research with a major industrial engineering enterprise. He looked forward to applying his theoretical expertise to written reports, analytical research and only occasional times for informal sharing of ideas, over lunch or late in the day before going home to a solitary evening with his own thoughts. This sequence of events not being immediately evident on accepting the job, he found that most of his available time was spent in lengthy meetings, in which he had to participate and could not ruminate on theoretical issues. These meetings created in him extreme aversion, to such a point that he developed physical symptoms, which caused him, more often than not, to excuse himself from these meetings, to the detriment of his job performance. *Clarification and development of the problem.*

He *accordingly* requested a change in assignment and was placed on a research team that he thought would be involved only in research. However, he soon found that this research team was the spearhead of the company's product development program. This involved the preparation and delivery of weekly presentations to potential customers and related enterprises. These presentations totally unnerved him, and after a serious and very public breakdown, he was relieved of this responsibility as well. *Changes caused by the problem.*

This was the primary reason he decided to get a different job altogether. He carefully prepared a resumé and collected various types of documentation. Now came the time to be interviewed. While he had no difficulty writing letters to potential employers, he could not accept even one interview, so devastated was he psychically at the prospect. *A specific problem occasioned by a new option.*

By exploring his predilictions openly and critically, he *ultimately* learned to accept his limitations and began to plan for any and all alternatives available for his career expertise. The first effect of this acceptance and exploration was a feeling of peace. As he persevered in his research, he began to enjoy a feeling of hope and possibility. After several weeks of cogitation, he reached the perfect solution. He would write about his hindrances, and so share with others what he had learned. *Personal responses to the problem and a solution.*

Classification Essay

- A classification essay tells how items, ideas and concepts can be sorted into different categories. to help explain their meaning.

- The thesis statement should explain the characteristics and the significance of each category.

- The topic sentence should briefly introduce the items, ideas or concepts to be classified.

- The introductory paragraph should identify the specific categories into which the items, ideas or concepts are to be classified.

- Each category should have enough detail to show how it is different from the other categories.

- The arrangement of categories should befrom least important to most important.

Essay Outline

Introductory Paragraph
Topic Sentence_____
Thesis Statement_____

Body Paragraph 1
Category 1_____
_____

Body Paragraph 2
Category 2_____
_____

Body Paragraph 3
Category 3_____
_____

Concluding Paragraph
Concluding Statement (*summarizes and repeats introductory ideas, makes a prediction, gives advice, makes a suggestion*)
_____
_____

Steps in Writing a Classification Essay

*Choose a topic from the list below and identify the possible categories.
Make a chart of categories with specific items, ideas or concepts arranged into each category.
List the categories in order of importance, with specific ideas.
Organize an outline from your chart of categories as shown on the previous page.*

Transitions for Classification Essays

one kind	the final type	certainly	in the same way
the first category	the next part	indeed	in contrast
one way	the first group	in essence	similarly
the main group	for example	in particular	while
another kind	for instance	although	for the most part
the last group	as an illustration	as a result	generally
another way	above all	at the same time	in general
the least	after all	even so	on the whole

Topic Possibilities

Cars
Careers
Educational opportunities
Universities
City sights
Personalities
Government styles
Cultures
Courses for majors
Modes of transportation
Fiction & non-fiction
News reports

Economic systems
Political systems
Raising children
Religion
Personal philosophies
Great philosophers
Great leaders
Emperors & kings
Democracy
The representative republic
Monarchy
Tyranny

Assessment for Classification Essays

Does the introduction **identify** the things, ideas or concepts to be classified?
Does the thesis statement indicate the **important categories** to be discussed?
Does each topic sentence clearly identify the **category** discussed in the paragraph?

Are the categories clearly **delineated** in the essay?
Is the **language convincing** throughout the essay?
Are the categories and their components clear and **accessible**?

Model Classification Essay

The Narcissistic Personality

Narcissism is a personality disorder in which a person is obsessed with conflicts about personal adequacy, power, prestige and vanity. The narcissitic personality usually reacts to critical appraisal and perceived rejection with anger. Other symptoms include a high opinion of the self accompanied by fantasies of exaggerated power. A narcissist has difficulty relating to others because of a lack of empathy and an exaggerated sense of self-worth. *Explanation of characteristics of narcissism.*

One kind of narcissism derives from excessive admiration, unbalanced by realism. Excessive praise and over-valuation by parents is as significant in developing narcissism as is unpredictable parental caregiving. Narcissistic personality disorder results from a belief that the individual is unacceptably flawed. For this reason, he tries to exert control over the views and behavior of others. *Explanation of causes of narcissism.*

Another kind of narcissism, pathological narcissism, can result from impaired familial relationships. As a result, the individual perceives himself as unimportant and unconnected to other people. Consequently, he becomes controlling and self-absorbed, blaming others for every problem. He develops an inability to deal with difficulty or criticism. His perceived fantastical image of his own grandiosity makes it difficult for him to work cooperatively with others. *Details of some of the symptoms of narcissism.*

The final type of narcissistic personality disorder is malignant narcissism. In this form of narcissism, the person is lacking in conscience and has difficulty controlling his behavior. Schizoid symptoms can predominate and a heightened sense of paranoia is in evidence. Various psychologists have characterized this form of narcissism as evil and a the root of inhumanity. Others have suggested that it is a denial of reality in an attempt to escape from frustration. In the idealization of the ego, the resultant sense of grandiosity can become aggressive and hence destructive. *Description of the most extreme form of narcissism.*

One way to treat the various types of narcissisitic personality disorder includes hospitalization to stabilize behavior. Other patients need the support of residential care. Cognitive behavioral therapy can replace destructive traits with healthier ones. Family therapy can help solve problems through exploration of conflicts and through communication with patients. Group therapy can help develop better interpersonal relationships by listening to others, understanding their feelings, and extending support. Although there is no medication to treat narcissistic personality disorder, the forms of treatment mentioned above can alleviate some of the most destructive symptoms. *Description of treatment possibilities.*

Process Essay

- A process essay describes how something works or how to do something in separate clear and important steps.

- The topic sentence should identify both the process itself and/or clear directions as well as the reason for the essay.

- The steps of the process and the directions are explained clearly in the correct order, from beginning to end.

- The essay desribes the cautions that are to be taken, and the length of the process, as well as possible variations in outcomes.

- The importance of each step is emphasized, as well as the difficulties that can be encountered.

- The needed skills and equipment for the process are clearly defined and explained.

Essay Outline

Introductory Paragraph
Topic Sentence_____
Thesis Statement_____

Body Paragraph 1
Step 1_____
_____

Body Paragraph 2
Step 2_____
_____

Body Pargraph 3
Step 3_____
_____

Concluding Paragraph
Concluding Statement (*summarizes and repeats introductory ideas, makes a prediction, gives advice, makes a suggestion*)
_____
_____

Steps in Writing a Process Essay

Choose a process from the list below that you understand very well.
Create an outline, stating the steps in the correct sequence, or in order of importance.
Decide which steps need further explanation or interpretation.
Create an outline as in the chart on the previous page.

Transitions for Process Essays

after a few hours	eventually	in the end	meanwhile
afterwards	finally	in the future	next
at last	first, second, third	in the meantime	soon after
at the same time	first of all	in the meanwhile	previously
before	formerly	last	simultaneously
before this	immediately before	last but not least	subsequently
currently	immediately after	lastly	then
during	initially	later	in the long run

Topic Possibilities

Making a meal	Improving a course
Changing a tire	Driving defensively
Planning a party	Succeeding at a job interview
Buying a car	Showing appreciation
Planning a vacation	Holding a yard sale
Buying a house	Choosing a marriage partner
Riding a bicycle	Looking fashionable on a limited budget
Taking a driving test	Falling into debt
Planning a presentation	How to meet more people
Using a smartphone	How bad habits develop
Making a quilt	Getting over a disappointment
Deciding on a major	Being a responsible pet owner

Assessment for Process Essays

Does the introduction identify the process to be described or the **directions** to be explained?
Does the thesis statement clarify the the **purpose** of the essay?
Is every **necessary step** included in the correct order, and with explanations?

Does the topic sentence clearly identify *major stages* in the process?
Are the directions clear and **succinct**, making the steps clear to the reader?
Is the **order** of the process explained logically and coherently?

Model Process Essay

- 🟩 Topic/thesis statements
- 🟦 Transitions
- 🟥 Paragraph descriptions

Quilting Bee

On Saturday mornings we gather for quilting. This is a weekly ritual we totally enjoy. First, we have coffee and share the events of the week. Very soon, we settle down around the table and begin to discuss our project for the day. Each week we make further progress as we define what the next step is and who should be responsible for each of the separate tasks. With laughter and great pleasure, we begin. *General introduction to the process of quilting together.*

Before we began the current project, we had selected a quilt block pattern and during the week we had purchased the different fabric patterns and colors for our block and edging design. Today is the day for careful cutting. While some of us watch, others take turns preparing the fabric layers and placing them on the cutting mat. The rotary cutter flies across the fabric and soon we have uncountable pattern pieces to stitch together. *Description of the first step.*

Several of us have meanwhile set up the sewing machines, each with a quilting foot and matching colored threads. Soon the whir of the machines drowns out our chatter as we assiduously stitch together the varied pattern pieces into one beautifully designed block. Hours later the assembly is complete and we lay out the blocks to judge how they should be put together in our quilt arrangement. That job is soon complete and we eagerly anticipate the assembly stage, since now our work will gain definition and true beauty. *Description of the assembly process.*

As soon as we are satisfied with our arrangement, we begin to stitch the individual blocks together in the agreed-upon pattern. Then we carefully stitch the quilt top to the batting and then to the backing. Now begins the final process - the top stitching to further design the surface for beauty and to combine the designed fabric layer with the batting and backing layer for stability. We use assorted patterns to guide our stitching. Today's quilt, because of its small size, can be machine-quilted, but often, when we make a larger quilt, we stretch the quilt on a frame and handstitch it together through the several layers. *Explanation of the final process.*

While quilt-making is time-consuming, it provides us with great pleasure and satisfaction as we, week after week, produce another work of art that will delight the person who receives it, or the one who purchases it for personal use or to give to a loved one. In the long history of quilting, the practice of working together is a tradition that has survived time. We relish our Saturday morning get-togethers, during which we not only socialize, but also produce works of lasting charm and beauty. *Summary of group quilt efforts.*

Answer Key

Answer Key

Nouns & Articles

1. devices — companies
2. paths — trails
3. books
4. flowers — flower
5. house — house
6. cars — car
7. concerts — plays
8. trees — traffic
9. suitcases — luggage
10. no article — no article
11. the
12. the — the
    a — an
    the
13. no article — no article
    no article — no article
    no article — no article
    no article — no article
14. no article — no article
    no article — a
15. a — a/the
    a — a
    the — the
    the

Verbs & Tenses

1. are studying
   are also studying
   are held
2. studied
   had already attended
   began
3. always attend
   study
   go
   read
4. attend
   called
   not reach
   were attending

Verbs & Tenses (continued)

5. finished
   are taking
   have been
   intend
   have taken
   have ever taken
6. experiences
   have experienced
   will experience
7. began
   have occurred
   causes
8. showed
9. tell
   say
   cause
10. depends
11. know
    cannot accurately foretell
    will be
12. happened
    struck
    were riding
    working
    studying
    changed
    were swept
    drowned
13. were swept
    never seen
    died
14. predict
    depend
15. often cause
    allow
    reaches
    had been
    have been
16. seem

Answer Key

Adjectives

1. *Answers can vary*
   A tornado is as dangerous as a hurricane.
   A tornado is not as dangerous as a hurricane.
   A hurricane is as dangerous as a tornado.
   A hurricane is not as dangerous as a tornado.
2. A pond is not as big as a lake.
3. *Answers can vary*
   In my opinion, playing soccer is as exciting as watching a soccer match.
   In my opinion, playing soccer is not as exciting as watching a soccer match.
   In my opinion, watching a soccer match is as exciting as playing soccer.
   In my opinion, watching a soccer match is not as exciting as playing soccer.
4. *Answers can vary*
   more beautiful
   more wonderful
   more awesome
   more amazing
5. A puddle is smaller than a pool.
   A pool is bigger (larger) than a puddle.
6. A river is wider than a brook.
   A brook is narrower than a river.
7. Walking along a country lane is as relaxing as sitting in a garden on a quiet summer day.
   Sitting in a garden on a quiet summer day is as relaxing as walking along a country lane.
8. Sitting on a park bench is not as comfortable as sitting in an easy chair.
9. Hiking along a path is not as difficult as climbing a mountain.
10. brighter
11. happier
12. harder
    wetter
13. the most beautiful
14. the most exhausted
15. the deepest ocean
16. the highest mountains on earth
17. the most popular form of entertainment
18. the biggest
    more people

Adverbs

1. Carly doesn't often play volleyball.
2. He doesn't usually have to work late.
3. Josh is going to Spain and he is also going to Portugal.
4. Jane frequently goes shopping on Saturday.
5. I can never remember to bring my books to class.
6. I have seen them at baseball games, but I have never spoken to them.
7. If we hadn't taken the same class, we would (never) have never met.
8. It hasn't stopped snowing yet.
9. The haven't finished repairing the roof yet.
10. The children haven't woken up yet.
11. Ann hasn't found a new apartment yet.
12. I haven't decided what to do yet.
13. The plane hasn't left yet.
14. anywhere
15. there   downstairs
    up   down
    everywhere

Answer Key

Adverbs (continued)

16. next week
17. soon
18. usually
19. hardly
20. barely
21. really
22. almost
23. They are still sleeping.
24. I hve already finished.
25. She seldom practices.

Sentence Structure

1. Tara not only went to see a movie, but also went to dinner afterwards.
2. She tried to pass the test, yet she failed.
3. Neither Tara nor her boyfriend went to see the movie.
4. The reports were all mixed up on the desk; therefore we couldn't find the right report when we needed it.
   The resports were all mixed up on the desk. Therefore we couldn't find the right report when we needed it.
5. I have an idea that we should consider; it might help us solve our problems.
   I have an idea that we should consider. It might help us solve our problems.
6. The icicles were melting; the brass bucket caught the freezing drops of water.
   The icicles were melting. The brass bucket caught the freezing drops of water.

Sentence Structure (continued)

7. Look for hummingbirds around that tree; they've been nesting.
   Look for hummingbirds around that tree. They've been nesting.
8. b
9. a
10. a
11. b
12. c
13. a
14. c

Transitions

1. b
2. c
3. a
4. c
5. c
6. c
7. a
8. c
9. c
10. c
11. a
12. c
13. a

Modifiers

1. Sweating in the humid sunshine, the tennis players bounced the balls back and forth across the tennis court.
2. Exhausted after the long day at work, we finally spent our time relaxing.
3. Made by my niece, the vase full of flowers brightened the room.
4. The book that I borrowed from you last week kept me awake all night.

Answer Key

Modifiers (continued)

5. A small reflecting pool filled with goldfish surrounded the ancient temple.
6. Snow began to fall heavily as it became starkly colder.
7. Though she was only aged ten, the modeling agency awarded her the contract.
8. Science students find frogs, green, slimy amphibians with bulbous noses, extremely interesting.
9. I witnessed a tsunami hitting the shore with the sound of thunder and splashing of water.
10. As we went further westward toward the ocean, the scenery became more and more beautiful.
11. Although we were totally exhausted, the party was so good that we stayed all night.
12. Last weekend we were snowed in by a terrible blizzard angrily blowing from north to south.
13. b
14. b
15. a
16. a
17. a
18. c
19. a

Gerunds & Infinitives

1. to take
2. looking
   to stop
3. to take
4. walking
5. to ask
   to call
   going
   dancing

Gerunds & Infinitives (continued)

6. to ask
   to tell
   to remember
   to bring
7. playing/*answers can vary*
8. taking
9. making
10. listening
11. playing
12. b
13. a
14. b, c
15. *answers can vary*
16. *answers can vary*
17. *answers can vary*
18. *answers can vary*
19. *answers can vary*
20. to come
21. to lend
22. answers can vary
23. answers can vary
24. answers can vary
25. having/to have
26. to take
27. answers can vary
28. getting
    answers can vary
29. answers can vary
30. (a) S
    (b) D
    (c) D
    (d) S

Prepositions

1. to
2. with
3. of
4. about
5. to
   to
6. from

Answer Key

Prepositions (continued)

7. to
8. for
9. with
10. about
11. with
12. for
13. to
    from
14. about
    in
15. from
16. in
17. at
18. to
    about
19. from
20. of
21. to
    with
22. for
23. with
24. for
    at
25. with
    about
26. about
27. to
    for
28. for
29. on
30. to
31. from
32. on
33. from
34. on
35. about
36. for
37. to
38. on
39. about
40. of
41. about

Prepositions (continued)

43. for
44. to

Phrasal Verbs

1. putting on
2. put it back
3. putting off
4. put/off
5. woke/up
6. put/on
7. called on
8. ran into
9. got over
10. put on
11. looked up
    wrote/down
12. figure/out
13. put/on
14. wrote/down
15. looked/up
16. put/off
17. pick/up
18. ran into
19. throw/out
20. made/up
21. turn/up
22. tried/on
23. hung/up
24. put/away
25. turned/over
    looked/on
26. go over
    filled/out
27. fill up
28. tore/up
29. tore/down
30. printed out
3. turn around
   go back

Answer Key

Phrasal Verbs (continued)

32. crossed/out
33. go/over
34. print/out

Forms

1. do
2. make
3. did
4. making
5. doing
6. making
7. made
8. make
9. made
10. did
11. make
12. do
13. made
14. do
15. done
16. do
17. make
18. do
19. took off
20. taking on
21. take/back
22. take/back
23. take a break
24. take a rest
25. getting over
26. gets cold
27. getting
28. gets
29. get
30. get along
31. gets me
32. gets upset
33. get
34. get
35. got
36. get
37. get to visit

Forms (continued)

38. get
39. gotten
40. get
41. get
    get

Clauses

1. As soon as the commissioner arrives, we'll start the meeting.
2. After I borrowed the book from the library, I read it quickly.
3. Whenever he visits different companies, he gives many excellent presentations.
4. Just as we were leaving for Honolulu, we got the news about the free trip.
5. They had to stay overnight at the airport until the weather cleared up.
6. The first time I went jet-skiing in Hawaii, I felt exhilarated.
7. Now that we have completed the required courses, we can continue studying for our degree.
8. Since the wather had been inclement all week, we decided to postpone the beach party.
9. The language course was very difficult for him because he had not done the preliminary work.
10. *Answers can vary*
11. *Answers can vary*
12. *Answers can vary*
13. b
14. b
15. a
16. b
17. b
18. You can't visit other countries and return to your own country officially unless you have a passport.

Answer Key

Clauses (continued)

19. Noone can remain in good health unless they eat healthy food and do exercises.
20. We won't go walking in the park unless you want to.
21. You can't ever get into the soccer stadium for any match unless you buy a season ticket.
22. I won't be able to buy a new car unless I get a good job.

Parallel Structure

1. b
2. a
3. a
4. b
5. a
6. b
7. b
8. a
9. the audience didn't want to listen to him
10. spend the day having fun
11. in the evening, watching
12. I don't enjoy
13. whether I feel worse
14. a
15. c
16. b
17. a
18. a

Sentence Variety

1. a
2. b
3. b
4. b
5. b
6. a
7. a
8. b
9. a
10. a
11. a
12. b
13. a
14. b
15. a

Sentence Expansion Example
The weather was cold and the wind relentless. It had been snowing heavily for days, and the hills and fence posts were covered with an ever-deepening blanket of snow that threatened to obliterate the entire landscape with its density and its weight...

Idiomatic Expressions

1. easy does it
2. basket case
3. get the hang of it
4. icing on the cake
5. in a fog
6. left in the dark
7. made in the shade
8. no laughing matter
9. on a roll
10. pain in the neck
11. piece of cake
12. quiet before the storm
13. read between the lines
14. taken aback
15. waters
16. fire
17. in the air
18. a fine line
19. a storm
20. board
21. to the wall
22. it a day
23. in stone
24. the ball rolling
25. b

Answer Key

Idiomatic Expressions (continued)

26. a
27. b
28. b
29. b
30. a
31. a
32. a
33. b
34. b

Phrases

1. a
2. b
3. g
4. b
5. c
6. f
7. d
8. e
9. walking steadily uphill…the hikers
10. playing until the sun had set…the children
11. disappointed…the young couple
12. worried about the approaching storm…the people at the picnic
13. blowing eerily around the house…the wind
14. her manner expressing her great disappointment
15. their shouts of laughter filling the air
16. her senses filled with wonder
17. shouting loudly, their voices shrill in the stillness, their breaths icy in the cold, their hair streaming in the wind
18. her long straight hair blowing in the breeze, her mood ruminative and distant, the dog asleep at her feet
19. his hair and clothing drenched

Resources

englishpage.com

Tutorials & Interactive exercises

- Verb tenses
- Conditionals
- Modals
- Gerunds
- Prepositions

Extensions

Reading Room
- Newspapers
- Magazines
- Books
- Reference

Listening Lounge
- NPR
- BBC

EnglishClub.com

Tutorials & Interactive exercises

- Listening
- Speaking
- Reading
- Writing

Extensions

Videos

grammar.ccc

Guide to Grammar & Writing

Explanations & Interactive exercises

- Word & Sentence Level
- Paragraph Level
- Essay & Research Paper Level

SentenceSense.com

ebook in basic writing

Tutorials & Interactive exercises

Part 1: How Sentences Work
Part 2: Common Writing Errors
Part 3: Techniques & Topics

UsingEnglish.com

- Idioms
- Phrasal Verbs
- Quizzes
- Language Tests
- Reading Comprehension
- Essay Samples

owl.english.purdue.edu

- Online Writing Lab
- Exercises
- MLS Formatting & Style
- APA Formatting & Style

contact@englisheditingessentials.com

Online Advice

- Questions
- Editing
- Support

Contact us with any questions
We can edit your essays and reports
We offer language support at any level

www.ingramcontent.com/pod-product-compliance
Lightning Source LLC
Chambersburg PA
CBHW041510220426
43661CB00047B/1521